Beginning Saint

Beginning Saint

Living 24 Hours a Day in the Consciousness of Your Highest Self

Carol Fabric

Beginning Saint Press

Cover design by Laura Ostrowski

Beginning Saint Press
21 Encina Place
San Anselmo, Ca 94960
(415) 721-7864
www.beginningsaint.com

ISBN: 9780983749103

Printed in the United States of America

I dedicate this book to my mother, Geraldine,

my children, Joie and Mia,

my godchildren, Michelle, Eric, Ram, Emmanuel,

and the Beginning Saint within each of you.

Letter to My God Children

My dearest Joie, Mia, Mary, Tania, Tim, Michelle, Eric, Peyton, Preston, Ram, Emmanuel, Madeline, Melanie, Jennifer, Thomas, and everyone unnamed,

As your mother, sister, godmother and auntie, my responsibility is to help you make sense of this planet and your life. Seekers of Truth down through the ages have shouted out to the heavens: "Who am I? Why am I here? What am I supposed to do here on earth?"

These are the most important questions of your life, and I pray you keep asking them until you find the answers that resonate with what feels true inside you. The saints tell us, "Listen to the still, small voice of your own true Self."

Your inner voice is your direct, wireless connection to God, who resides within you and exists as you. A friend of mine says, "The good thing about our conversation with God is that it's always a local call."

When you train yourself to listen, you will be able to discriminate between any limited ideas of who you are and the truth of your own higher, unlimited Self. You will develop increasing power over old limiting attitudes and beliefs and will fall in love with your true Self.

You are already a "beginning saint," a saint in process, who can become fully awake in this very lifetime. You can become a "*jivanmukta*," the Sanskrit word for one who is "liberated while still in a human body."

What does that mean? A jivanmukta is a person who lives with the understanding of a saint in his or her everyday life. Because he knows who he truly is, a *jivanmukta* is free from fear, and all his actions spring from the highest good.

My wish for you is to realize your own greatness and live in the joy of knowing who you really are.

Table of Contents

You're It

God
Disguised
As a myriad things and
Playing a game
Of tag

Has kissed you and said,
"You're it—

I mean, you're Really IT!"

Now
It does not matter
What you believe or feel

For something wonderful,

Major-league Wonderful
Is someday going
To

Happen.

-Hafiz

The Gift

Introduction

My Grandmother

My beloved one-hundred-five-year-old Grandmother was dying in a hospital in Jackson, Mississippi. I flew back to Mississippi to be with her in her final hours, buoyed by my Bible, *The Tibetan Book of Living and Dying*, a copy of the "Twenty-third Psalm," assorted chants, poems and songs….all with the intention of helping my grandmother to die. "Nana" had gathered her family around her and had telephoned her goodbyes to friends and grandchildren who could not be there.

The doctors told us that it would be "any time now"—that all her "systems" were failing. She said to the group of us standing by her bed, "Well, I'm going to die now." She laid her head back on her pillow and started to breathe in the way I'd heard that dying people breathe.

Family members tearfully filed out of the room, leaving me and Nana to perform the rituals and say the goodbyes that allow the soul to peacefully leave the body and move into the next dimension. I sat by her side, sang my favorite chant to her, and prayed for her happy departure.

Inspired to help her die, at one point I took the oxygen tube out of her nose. A few moments later the doctor walked into the room. Feeling I might have done something wrong, I said to him, "If she's still breathing in forty-five minutes I'll put it back in." He nodded and said, "As a physician I can't do it, but if you want to, I think it's okay." He respectfully left the room and I continued to say prayers for Nana.

Forty-five minutes later Nana was still breathing, so I gently slipped the oxygen tube back into her nose and continued offering her rounds of chants and prayers.

Half an hour later Nana sat straight up in bed and demanded in an angry tone of voice, "Get me some iced tea."

Totally startled, I said, "Sure, Nan."

Suddenly feeling hysterical inside and not knowing whether to laugh or cry, I handed her the iced tea and just looked at her in amazement. Shaking her head from side to side, and with a disgusted look on her face, she said, "This is so embarrassing, everyone in Michigan thinks I'm dead. But I can't die now, I don't know where I'm supposed to go!"

Hearing her plea, I felt like crying myself. There was my Nana, one hundred five years old—in that moment she had no clue how to let go of her wonderful body and move on.

She wasn't ready.

Two days later she was released from the hospital, went home and lived another six months. She was totally awake and aware at one hundred five and a half when she finally, peacefully, let go of her body.

I don't know spiritually what happened in that six months that allowed Nana to finally take the leap. What did she discover? What choice did she make that allowed her to move into the next dimension?

What I do know is that it inspired me to ask myself, "Carol, why wait until death is upon you or a loved one to find out who you really are and what this life is all about?"

All over the world, young and old alike are seeking answers to these same questions.

I Can't Die Now

My daughters were eleven and thirteen when I discovered I had a brain tumor. I had never known anyone to survive a brain tumor, so, like my Nana, I cried out to the universe, "I can't die now! Not before I learn why I am here in the first place!"

The universe answered me pretty quickly, to say the least. Soon after the diagnosis, my dearest friend, Elizabeth, called. "How are you doing Carol?" she asked.

"I could use some peace of mind," I replied.

"I'll bring it right over," she offered gently.

Within minutes, Elizabeth was on my doorstep with a book by the East Indian saint Swami Muktananda, *The Play of Consciousness*. In it he addressed all of the questions I had been asking myself for years. I read it voraciously cover to cover. From one page to another I remember nodding to myself, "Yes, yes, yes. This is what I want to know!"

By the end of the week I had tracked down Swami Muktananda and flown to Miami, where I found him teaching and initiating students into meditation. His two primary teachings were: 1) God dwells within you as you. 2) See God in each other.

I had been raised in a spiritual tradition that, like many, taught two incompatible teachings: 1) God is everywhere. 2) Never go to doctors.

In this tradition, it was God who did the healing, not the doctors, and, at that time, although I believed that "God is everywhere," to me, "everywhere" was somewhere "out there." "Everywhere" could not possibly include in doctors … or in me or you.

At one point during Muktananda's meditation Intensive, students were invited to personally meet the saint. My husband, Bruce, said, "Carol, go up to the front of the room and ask Muktananda to heal you."

I thought, if Muktananda is who his students say he is—a true saint, an enlightened being like Jesus—he would already know why I was there.

"You go," I replied.

Bruce walked up to the front of the room, bowed with respect to the seventy-two-year-old wise man, and asked, "My wife has a brain tumor. What should we do?"

When Bruce returned to the back of the room where I was sitting, I pounced on him, "What did he say? What did he say?"

Bruce replied, "He said you should pay attention to the doctors."

On hearing that, I became really angry, "I just flew three thousand miles and spent all this money just to meet a man who supposedly can heal me of this brain tumor. If he really *is* all-knowing, he would know I'm not supposed to go to doctors!"

Bruce had had enough of me. He proceeded to walk away and let me stew in my own juices. I sat there for a long time. I was desperate, "I'd better think this through," I thought.

I decided to have a conversation with myself: "Okay, Carol, let's just suppose for a moment that what they tell you about the saint is true. Let's suppose that he can read your mind. Let's say he does know who you really are and what you believe. If that were true, what would this enlightened saint tell you?"

All of a sudden I started to cry. I realized that a teacher who truly knows that God is everywhere and within everyone, would say exactly what Muktananda did say, "Pay attention to the doctors."

He would know that, of course, God exists within doctors, that God exists in medicine, in all people, in everyone, in everything and in every place, and in all universes and beyond.

With my inner understanding confirmed and my fears gone, I flew home to San Francisco and arranged to be operated on by one of the best brain surgeons in the world. He zipped out the lemon-sized mass and I was back to work in two weeks.

In your own life you may be doing just fine, with no major upsets or illnesses to sabotage your goals. Many of your life's dreams may already have been realized.

Yet you may be searching for more. Deep inside, you may know that this life is meant for something far greater, something much more profound and meaningful than you have known before. You may feel compelled to find out what that is for you, and find yourself leaving the comfort of your known world to journey into a whole new realm of understanding.

In My Office

A young woman slid slowly down onto my couch and began to cry. I asked my usual opening question. "And what brings you here today, my dear?" She gasped, trying to hold back her tears. "I don't know. I just don't know anything. I mean, I know my name, I know my friends and family, my address, but who am I really? I have no idea. What am I supposed to be doing here? I'm taking college courses, but they don't mean anything to me."

Stunned, I paused for a moment, then listened more carefully. What was she really saying?

Was she asking herself, "What am I doing in this therapist's office today?" Was she going to tell me how depressed she was, about the loss of a love relationship, how she was doing poorly in school, or was not able to concentrate or get along with her parents?

Was she going to tell me she'd been raped, abused, was pregnant or addicted?

Her reply to every question I posed was, "No, not that; no, not that; no, not that."

Then I asked, "Do you mean, *"Who am I, what am I doing in this body, living in Silicon Valley, California, on the planet earth*?"

She sat up straight, looked directly into my eyes, and said, "Exactly."

Over and over I had heard clients express the same inner struggle. Each time my heart was gripped, "How can I offer clients an experience of what I know?"

Each client was reaching out for answers to important life questions, but each had little basic understanding from which to look. Their fabulous educations had not taught them how their minds actually work, how life works, how to navigate relationships, or especially how to recognize and value their own exquisite selves.

From generation to generation true saints have carried the key: *You are It. You are God.* They tell us that the purpose of life is to discover your great Self, your God-Self, your eternal, truly limitless, boundless loving nature, your infinite creativity, and your ever-growing, multifaceted powers. They tell us that when you consciously learn how to use your innate powers, you will be able to create a life that grows every day in joy and meaning.

I wrote *Beginning Saint* to offer you many of their spiritual teachings, and especially those that make the most sense to me. My wish is that this book will ignite your own longing for the Truth.

PART I

Only the Self can know the Self.
Only God can know God.
You are that Self.
You are that God.

—Swami Muktananda
To Know the Knower

Chapter 1

The Biggest Questions of Your Life

The one essential and ancient teaching taught by the enlightened saints of every major spiritual and philosophical tradition is:

God Is Everywhere

Saints teach that the foundation of all true knowledge is *"God is everywhere"*—that this Presence exists in and through all forms, all people and all conditions. In every church, temple, mosque and synagogue, somewhere painted on a wall or printed in a text will be the message, *"God is everywhere."* How many of you have taken this message seriously?

You may have thought, "Oh yes, I know God is everywhere," but never really contemplated what this teaching ultimately means or how to apply it in your life.

True enlightened saints tell us *God is everywhere*, including in you and me. They tell us, "There is no place where God is not." Many spiritual traditions teach, *God is everywhere*, but they mean, God, the Cosmic Creator of the entire universe exists everywhere, but NOT actually within you.

You have probably heard the teaching many times throughout your life, but possibly you believed it meant, "God surrounds everything but couldn't possibly live within me personally, and it's a cinch God does not reside in this or that person."

A Child's View

One day, at age two and a half, my precocious daughter Joie arrived home from church with her grandparents. She was all bubbly and happy, and I decided to engage her in a conversation about God. I asked her, "Tell me sweetheart, what did you learn in Sunday school today?"

She thought for a moment, then very seriously replied, "We talked about the significance of sin."

I was amused that she used such a big word at her age, so trying to keep from laughing and attempting to take her more seriously, I repeated back to her, "What *is* the significance of sin?"

She stood there thinking about it for a few moments. Then all of a sudden she lit up. "Cin … Cin … Cinderella!" she shouted joyfully.

I realized in that moment that, like me, Joie had probably picked up some misunderstandings at church and would undoubtedly have to sort out the Truth for herself.

Joie's father and I, recognizing parenting as a spiritual practice, found our selves forced to clarify our own spiritual convictions in order to help Joie become clear about hers.

In past generations, ministers, rabbis, imams and priests taught that we are created by God and that we are close to God, but most did not teach us that we *are* God.

My friend Margot, raised in the Catholic tradition, said that her second-grade catechism book started out with the question, "Where is God?" The next page read, "God is everywhere." She told me that in her church growing up it was never okay to question the teachings. Margot recalled, "Discovering your own truth was never encouraged."

God is Everywhere

She said, "The teaching 'God is everywhere' was a great answer for a seven-year-old mind, but I never really contemplated the idea again, until twenty years later when I experienced a transforming breakthrough in understanding. I was so excited to finally understand that God really is everywhere, even in *me*. I had become able to understand it, not only intellectually, but also to experience the full power of it."

Young children automatically trust their parents and teachers, so it's easy for them to extend this same trust to the unseen God. When their parents teach them that there is a God, they simply assume God exists and have little difficulty talking to Him, even enlisting God as their best friend.

However, when they ask God for something and are let down, they often feel betrayed by the God of their understanding.

Tania was eleven when her father died of cancer. She told me she prayed over and over that he would get well. "When my dad died, I not only lost him, but experienced an even bigger loss. I lost God. I never trusted God again until I thought I might die myself."

Thousands of enlightened saints in all cultures have shared the teaching, *"I am That. I am God."* But up until now in the West this essential knowledge and experience has been kept a mystery. Some believed that if people actually knew they were God, they might use their powers in destructive ways.

Just the opposite has happened. Not knowing we are God living in a human form keeps us separate, afraid, and believing we are powerless.

Ignorance of this truth is at the center of our misunderstanding about ourselves, each other, and our world. Not knowing we are all equally *divine beings* has resulted in immeasurable suffering, even to this day. How many wars have been fought and are still being fought over beliefs about which group of people are the "chosen ones, the most right or the most good?"

It's easy to see how ignorance of the Truth, greed, fear, and misuse of power have managed to keep human beings from knowing their true identity, but this knowledge has never really been a secret.

Secret Shmeekret!

In our hearts, each of us has always known. So too, authentic saints have said for thousands of years *"You are God living a human life as the person you are."* True saints know who you are and for centuries have tried to tell you, "You're It! You are the Great Presence you've been looking for."

Although saints of every spiritual tradition in the world teach, *"God is everywhere,"* the true meaning of that teaching for so many of us has remained hidden. For so many, the search goes on.

In Louis Carroll's *Alice in Wonderland,* the caterpillar asks Alice, "Who-o-o Are You-u-u?" The saints all know the caterpillar is asking her a far deeper question—THE question that is meant to remind each of us of our true Self, our sacred identity, and the purpose of our birth.

The Game of Life
God
Shining Out Into Form

Chapter 2

The Creation Story

Many cultures teach a similar Creation Story. My first meditation teacher was Alan Watts, one of the first westerners to bring Zen Buddhism to the United States in the 1970s. When students asked Alan what he believed, he shared the following story:

"The Great Creator, the Master Artist, whom we call God, decided to play a game of hide-and-seek with Himself. Like a jeweler who designs everything out of gold or a potter who makes unlimited creations out of clay, God created everything out of His very own essence.

God wanted to create a really wonderful game. Like any game, so the story goes, He needed to include freedoms and obstacles and the challenge of Self-discovery. So, like hiding a "key to the kingdom," just for the fun of the game He chose to hide within the human heart this secret: "Everyone and everything is really made of God-substance."

God knew that one day human beings would discover the wonderful truth that God is who they are. They would finally know that their true God-Self is omnipotent, omniscient, and omnipresent, and they would use their powers to create a wonderful culture of love here on Earth."

The two stories of creation that are predominant in western culture at this time are the theory of evolution and creationism.

Evolution is the scientific theory that proposes that life as we know it began with an enormous explosion about 14 billion years ago. Scientists call this the "Big Bang" theory. As the resulting gigantic energy fields and gases began to cool down, galaxies, solar systems, planets and atmospheres formed. Life as we currently understand it, on planet Earth, began in the form of one- and two-celled animals, and then evolved to more-and-more-complex life forms.

Believers in the creationist theory teach the literal story of creation described in the Bible's Book of Genesis—that in six days, out of nothing, God created everything at once, including animals and human beings. Creationists do not give credence to Darwin's theory "the evolution of the species."

Over the centuries where self-aware human beings have lived, stories have developed about what is real and what is not. Each culture has created its own mythology about existence.

Perhaps the scientific explanation of "evolution," the "creationist" version, and the myriad stories and beliefs existing in cultures worldwide, can all be understood as true—at different levels of human development and comprehension.

Historically there was a stage in the development of human awareness where humans believed that if they could not visually see the existence of something that it in fact did not exist.

Even today, many people have difficulty trusting that life exists beyond the physical body.

However, as human beings re-learn of their true nature—their "God-Self," individually they come to perceive and experience an expanded reality beyond their five senses. And they come to realize that they are in fact, eternal beings.

Today, with communication and travel connecting almost everyone, and with global availability of scientific and educational resources, people all over the world are starting to recognize the similarities of their cultural stories. Differences between us are dissolving as we learn we're all made of the same essential energy. We are beginning to notice we are more similar than different in every way.

Discovering You Are God

All true saints tell us, the kingdom of God is within—the great God-Self lies within you and is the Truth of who you are. Your God-Self is whole, unbroken and not damaged in any way. You are a perfect, individual, always connected creation of that same indefinable, infinite, unlimited and ever-expanding Divine Energy, God.

The ego is the *small self*. It's the part of you that you may call "Paula" or "Bill." Often your *small self* believes you are limited. It has judgments, rules, and expectations about how you and others should think and behave. The *small self* often hangs on to thoughts that are not really true about you in present time. It may contain all types of decisions, attachments, judgments, comparisons and fear.

The ego is transformed when you replace outdated beliefs of limitation with new knowledge of your true, powerful, eternal God-Self. The beginning saint in you learns to disarm limited or painful thoughts, and you discover your true nature as boundless and free.

Your higher self, your God-Self, is made of love and limitless joy. It is fearless, playful, inspired, profound, eternal and full of awe. You are the fountain of all creativity and contentment. You are the source of love. When you feel centered in your highest awareness—your God-Self, your mind is at rest. You experience your own perfection, and realize you are the embodiment of love.

The beginning saint in you experiences more and more of these delicious feelings. You recognize your God-Self as your ultimate "Home" in which all things already exist. God has not gone anywhere. God resides perfectly in you, as you.

The Creation Story as it exists across cultures can seem like merely a delightful story, until you recognize the Truth in it.

When you really experience that *You Are It*, your whole life is transformed. You joyfully realize the enormous importance of recognizing your God-Self, loving your God-Self, and mastering your inherent God-powers. You begin to have more love and understanding for others and to want them to know their great God-Self, too.

Who Do You Think You Are?

You were born with unlimited possibilities, but little by little your ideas of yourself were formed by your interactions with others and the world. Little by little you shaped a limited belief of who you are, and now at times you may feel quite separate from God. Today is the day to reclaim your rightful lineage—the God-Self you truly are.

Many people don't know they are totally made of God. In answer to the question "Who am I?" most reply with one of the following understandings:

1) I am my body. I am one of millions of bodies. I am separate from everyone else. I'm here to suffer and endure what life has for me. When this body wears out I will die. That will be the end of me.

2) I am my body. I am one of millions of bodies. I am separate from everyone else. I'm here to have a wonderful and

meaningful experience here on earth. My goal will be to make the most of this life by dedicating it to helping others. When this body wears out I will die. I will be happy that I used my life well. That will be the end of me.

3) I am God inhabiting a human body in this lifetime. I am here to feel great joy, to love and be loved by others, and to evolve and grow as an individual ray of God. I am here to see God in myself and in others, and to contribute my God-Self in the most uplifting way. I know I am not my body. When this body wears out, my spirit essence will continue to exist. I will merge with my own highest God-Self, where I can rest indefinitely, or choose another adventure in this or other realms—an even more magnificent life with new games and purposes.

The Truth Stayed Hidden for 2000 Years

In her book *Beyond Belief*, author Elaine Pagels, describes how the politics of the time shaped the Christian perspective of who God is:

> In approximately 180 AD, Irenaeus, Bishop of Lyons, declared that only Matthew, Mark, Luke, and John collectively, and only these gospels exclusively, constitute the whole gospel.

She goes on to say that Irenaeus had set out to destroy all the writings that interpreted Jesus' teachings differently. This would, Irenaeus believed, concentrate the power of Jesus' teachings in Ireneaus' own hands.

Among the first to be destroyed were the writings of the disciple Thomas, who had set down the lessons he'd learned first-hand from Jesus.

On hearing of Irenaeus' plan, the followers of Thomas hid Thomas' manuscripts in huge clay pots in caves near Nag Hammadhi, Egypt.

The manuscripts remained in the caves until 1945, when a peasant exploring the caves, Muhammad Ali, unexpectedly discovered the jars. Having no idea of the significance of their contents, he turned the jars over to the authorities.

It wasn't until forty years later that the Gospels of Thomas were obtained and translated by Dr. Pagels. She discovered:

> The authors of John and Thomas take Jesus' private teachings in sharply different directions. John taught that one experiences God "only through the Divine Light embodied in Jesus." However, certain passages in Thomas' gospel, kept secret for 2000 years, draw quite a different conclusion, "the Divine light Jesus embodied is shared by all humanity, since we are all made in the image of God."

Professor Pagels continues, "Thus Thomas expresses what would become a central theme of Jewish and a thousand years later of Christian mysticism: that God is hidden within everyone, although most people remain unaware of God's presence."

This interpretation of Jesus' teachings, Professor Pagels explains, was a major departure from the teachings of John, Matthew, Mark and Luke, whose Gospels had dominated Christian understanding for two thousand years: Jesus did not, Professor Pagels says, encourage his disciples to follow him, but encouraged them instead *to focus on their own inner knowing.*

In the same way, the goal of a beginning saint is to recognize and feel God's presence within his own self. When that happens, his life is transformed. He sees his God-Self as his own best friend, honoring his mind, heart, and highest intentions, and recognizes others' motives as essentially good, too. He feels less fearful, realizing that all substances in the universe are made of the same essential God-Energy. He recognizes that all animate and inanimate things are created by God and contain only God, including himself.

The beginning saint becomes aware of the paradox in believing that God is both everywhere and separate, and resolves this dualistic thinking by expanding her awareness to include both realities. She recognizes her own inner Self as God living and expressing as a human being. Her widening shift in perception helps her recognize not only that God lives within her, but also that God exists as her, and as each one of us. As her consciousness continues to expand, she experiences happy changes in all areas of her life.

The twentieth-century philosopher Kahlil Gibran explained this phenomenon when he wrote:

> The unity of all things
> exists in and beyond diversity,
> the awareness of the Oneness
> and connectedness of
> all things.
>
> -Kahlil Gibran
> *The Prophet*

Why Not Be Polite?

Everyone
Is God speaking.
Why not be polite and
Listen to
Him?

—Hafiz
The Gift

Chapter 3

The Enlightened Saints All Know the Answer

You are great! You are Divine! You are the Great Presence you've been looking for. You have always existed and you will always exist.

In this lifetime you have a body that is perfect for you, that gives you perfectly what you need for optimum growth as an individual ray of God. You have earned a human body after many great deeds of love, and as a beginning saint you are ready for the next step on your adventure to enlightenment. You've identified your goal: to know and experience your God-Self, your own greatness and actual divinity, twenty-four hours a day.

You are perfectly in the world and perfectly on your path right now: it's time for you to experience that you are *That Magnificence*. What an amazing life you've chosen!

"But, is that all I need to know?" you ask.

Yes, if you comprehend what "everywhere" means, what an amazing embodiment of power you are, and apply this understanding in your life.

This has been the problem all along. Many of us have accepted the interpretations of a few and have not really contemplated, for ourselves, the simple, straightforward teaching: *God is everywhere.*

Learning that you are God living as "Suzy" or "Jim" is a start, but what are God's characteristics? How do you recognize God? How do we see God in ourselves? How do we communicate directly with God? How does knowing intellectually *God is everywhere* become a real experience for us?

Once you become aware of the possibility that *God dwells within you as you*, it's important to open up a conversation with your own God-Self, which might go something like this:

"Hey God, why didn't you let me know you were there all along, living within me as me? And, not only that, God, they tell us you exist everywhere! When did you think I'd get around to finding that out?"

"While I've wallowed in my own misunderstanding, feeling alone, confused and disconnected, lifetime after lifetime, all along you've been within me and I didn't even know it. It's sort of like learning I've always had wings, but didn't know they were there, or how to use them."

"Come on now God, help me out!"

As you continue this conversation with your God-Self, you begin to discover the answers to your life's questions. You notice the lessons to be learned in the very process of living and the thousands of ways to apply the understanding of your own divinity. You begin to recognize lessons when they show up, and learn from them rather than blaming your parents or doubting your own greatness. You come to know that you are engaged in a superb life game.

In writing *Beginning Saint*, it was my intention to offer you, in simple terms, a set of "flying instructions" for this process.

Beginning Saint is about living as a saint in your own life, being the fully realized being that you truly wish to be. It's about learning what skills and knowledge are needed to become the loving, joyful, healthy, compassionate, free and happy spirit that is the saint within you.

Beginning Saint maps the steps to using your divinity powerfully and constructively. It offers a perspective of who you are and how you got here. It shows you how to recognize and experience your God-Self. It describes the only two obstacles to happiness, and teaches you how to use your mind and feelings to transcend them.

In later chapters you will learn how to use the "Beginning Saint Bridge," a major tool for transformation that will help propel you over the quicksand of your own old habits and beliefs, and others faulty messages, freeing you to build an ever greater and ever more uplifting life.

Getting to Know Your Own God-Self

How could there be a more important task in the universe than knowing who you are and how life works? You've been learning that who you really are is God, but equally essential is to learn what "being God" means. It's important to discover how to use your God powers in beneficial ways.

Many stories exist in spiritual traditions across the world describing a seeker's discovery—just in the nick of time—of the hidden gem in his own pocket—the revelation of a poor child that he's really the inheritor of a marvelous kingdom, or the transformation of the inner frog into a radiant prince.

You are learning that you already possess all of God's characteristics of love, intelligence, creativity, and power.

But what does each of these qualities encompass, and how will you use them for the highest good for yourself, your family, friends, community and world?

First of all, you need to know that God is called by many different names in the world's spiritual traditions. God is known by *Allah* in the Islamic tradition, *Brahman* in the Hindu tradition, *Vairocana* in Mahayana Buddhism, *Adi-Buddha* in the Tibetan Buddhist tradition, *Great Father* in the American Indian spiritual tradition, *Aten* and *The Goddess* in the ancient Egyptian world, and *Yaweh* in the Hebrew tradition.

God is also known as *Om, The Source, Qi, Chi, Shiva, Krishna* and *Christ Consciousness*, but each name of God ultimately means the same thing and embodies the same single essence of love.

Am I a Beginning Saint?

Exercise 1

How do you know you are a beginning saint?
Ask yourself which statements are true for you:

I want to think more positively about myself and others.

I want my life to make a constructive difference on the planet.

I feel I'm being protected and guided.

My heart fills with love for people.

I feel grateful to be alive.

Sometimes I feel great energy soaring up within me.

Sometimes I feel a great light within me.

I believe there is a reality beyond this planet Earth.

I want to feel happier and I want to help other people feel happier.

I want to know how to alleviate both emotional and physical pain.

I'd like to learn more about being a powerful person in the world.

I want to know how to recognize God in my own life.
I want to know how this Universe came into being.
I want to know my larger life's purpose.
How did I get the family and friends I have?
I want to know what happens to me when I die.
When I'm "stuck" in an upset, how can I rebalance my emotional state in peace?
I don't always agree with teachings I learned from my spiritual education, family, friends or school.
I want the whole subject of God to make sense to me.
I want to let go of resentments.
I want to forgive myself and others.
I want to know how to maintain a happy attitude all day.
I want to love, trust, and feel comfortable with myself.

If you answered, "yes" to any of these questions or statements, you are absolutely a beginning saint, or well on your way.

What Is a Saint, Anyway?

You may have learned that a saint is an intermediary between you and God, but a saint is much, much more.

Have you ever had a moment in your life when you felt so much happiness and love you thought you'd burst?

Maybe it was during your first kiss, when you caught your first fly ball, when you skied down a mountain, or when you understood a mathematics or chemistry formula or rode a wave all the way to shore.

Maybe it was at the birth of a child, or on meeting an old friend, or having the perfect solution seemingly magically appear.

Most of us have had brief moments of ecstasy, or challenging moments when we trusted our "inner knowing" and discovered that, yes, our inner knowing was right all along.

We'd give anything for more of such moments, and, the truth is, within each of us is an unlimited spectrum of joy, a micro-ray of the state of enlightenment, the state that is the everyday reality of a saint.

A saint is a human being who knows that he himself is actually a living form of God, the Source of all creation. He has discovered that all powers of the "Source-God" exist within him, and within you. He knows that his true identity, and yours, is also God, living as him or as you.

A saint's life purpose is to use her life to uplift herself and others, and to generate more love, kindness, creativity, and compassion on the planet. A saint never doubts either her own God-Self or your God-Self, no matter what feelings or appearances manifest before her.

A saint trusts that all possibilities exist within every human being, but he is also realistic. He knows that essential perceptual changes are needed by most people to stabilize the awareness and application of the unlimited creativity within all of us. He is an empathetic teacher who has compassion for human foibles.

A saint knows that she is free to assume any role in society. She knows that "all jobs are God's jobs," and that all people have the potential to become saints.

There have been saints who were kings and jesters, saints who were doctors, cobblers, mothers and dads, cooks and carpenters. Even some young children were famous saints.

Ernest Holmes, a great synthesizer of mystical spiritual traditions around the world, taught that one's ability to create is equal to his or her level of awakened consciousness. This means that the greater your understanding and application of truth, the more exquisite your creations will be.

When the world cries out, "Where are our leaders of absolute wisdom and integrity? Where are our heroes?" the saints reply, "Within you, within you."

To qualify for sainthood in many spiritual traditions, a person has to perform a series of miracles. Usually the miracle has to be some kind of event that demonstrates to others that the saint has the power to see or to know something impossible for the rest of us.

You yourself may have experienced many different kinds of events and synchronicities that you told your friends were "just plain miracles."

And each day you may experience at least one simple "miracle," like finding a parking place in an impossible city, meeting a friend you were just thinking about, or locating the money you needed at the perfect moment.

These inexplicable synchronicities may seem insignificant in the greater scheme of things, but, what about the time you contained an impulse to make a nasty comment, or transformed your angry thought into kindness or inspiration? What about the time you stopped yourself from making an assumption due to a person's gender or race? What about the time you were patient with someone crossing the street? What about the time you chose to be generous … just because?

These are examples of monumental miracles, the kinds of miracles that saints practice every day.

Acts of loving kindness such as these are the most important miracles for the future of the planet, because they evidence the profound transformation of consciousness that will bring that future into reality.

As you grow on your spiritual path, you will find yourself naturally developing abilities and powers that you've never before dreamed possible.

Literally anyone can become a saint—choosing to live in a natural state of joy all day long.

Greater works than I do, you will do also.

—John 14:12

Saints of the past, like Jesus, used their powers to demonstrate what is possible for each of us. A saint recognizes that all God's powers and characteristics have taken form within him or her. He lives in joy, breathes joy, and looks only at the perfection of God's play. She lives her life knowing she is one of the unlimited forms of God.

And the saint knows that all of us are capable of the same attainment.

After realizing we each are a manifestation of God, the next step is to learn how to let go of everyday thoughts and attitudes that block us from seeing and knowing our highest God-Self.

A Saint Is a Perfect Ray of God

The process of becoming a saint begins with seeing the divine within yourself… and then recognizing the divine in everyone.

The primary difference between a beginning saint and a fully realized saint is that as a beginning saint you may not know that the powers of God are within you and that you can learn to use them predictably in your everyday life.

You may find old, conflicting beliefs blocking you from using those amazing abilities inherent within you. You may believe that saints have to be "good" all the time and that this will be difficult.

You will come to understand, however, that although the saints have total freedom of choice, because their thoughts and actions emanate from the highest understanding, so will their actions bring forth the highest benefit for everyone.

Did you know that most saints have a wild sense of humor?

In fact, saints have been known to laugh all day long. Some people think that if they were saints they wouldn't have any fun. In fact, to an authentic saint this world is a pretty funny and delightful place.

Saints are happy, playful, and full of energy. They are lovers of all God's creation, lovers of human beings, and lovers of all life, including their very own selves. They are the embodiment of both play and compassion.

Saints see each of us as whole, perfect and full of light—a "saint in process."

If a saint appears limited in any way, it's because he or she has temporarily reminded himself or herself of an experience of limitation in order to teach others. Saints create games and obstacles for the sheer fun of self-discovery.

Saints also have the inner freedom to assume any role in society. They may choose to function from the perspective of one gender or another to conform to the human condition of male or female, but saints perceive themselves ultimately as beyond gender, beyond right and wrong, beyond good and bad, beyond up and down and past and future—beyond all opposites.

Saints are liberated from the belief of limitation in all its myriad forms, and because of this they are free from judging and constantly comparing themselves with other people and things.

However, they also are delighted by differences and enjoy their own and others' individuality.

A saint lives his life as God. He knows there is no particle, no atom, no cell or space where God is not. He sees the world as God's play, with nothing out of order, nothing wrong. He knows everything is unfolding in its perfect time and place. Imagine how that state of awareness feels!

The saint knows how to access the unlimited powers of her own God-Self. She is liberated from the belief that she is separate or different from God. She is free from the fear of birth and death, lack, illness and loss. She experiences steady peace of mind.

Saints Are Prototypes of Human Beings of the Future

Saints are human beings at their best. Saints are models for the coming race of people. They look at life differently. Saints know they are God living in an individual form, loving as God loves, thinking as God thinks, knowing as God knows, and they creatively and powerfully take action in the world from that awareness.

Saints know, "It's God that I am seeing. It's God that I am feeling. God is who I am. God is the 'I' who sees out of my eyes. It is God that I see in others. God takes the form of all things in the universe and all dimensions."

As a child I was taught, *God is everywhere,* but I never really understood and experienced it as the truth until I started to see with new eyes.

The great saint Swami Muktananda taught that if you don't like what you see,

> "Change the prescription of your glasses"
>
> —Swami Muktananda
> *Secret of the Siddhas*

When I first learned to see a person or situation from a more uplifting perspective, I experienced myself looking from my heart, not just my eyes. When I assumed the point of view that God *is* everywhere—in all people, in all places, all things and all circumstances—I learned to see from a more compassionate heart.

Sometimes I have to stretch my own thinking a bit when the "God-dogs" next door are howling for hours at a time, or the evening news has just delivered a very sad story. Now, when I'm having difficulty seeing God in myself or someone else, in an event or a situation, I know my job is to stretch more expansively … then I can always see God in that person or situation.

When I first learned to see God everywhere, I noticed everyone looked more beautiful. I found myself greeting every person as if he or she were a new puppy—eager, fragile, joyful, just wanting to love and be loved—just trying to make sense of this world, as we all are.

Now when I look from my heart, animals, trees, flowers—even inanimate things—feel alive. I can feel every obstacle, every lesson I receive, supporting me to live, grow, and be happy. The whole world appears brighter. My conscious self wakes up. I have moments feeling the kind of happiness that is independent of things or external forces—I feel happy, and a steady delight, in just being alive.

I've realized my ability to see God depends only on the sweetness of my heart at any given time, and on being able to shift my thoughts beyond my cultural programming.

Teachings of the Poet Saints

The poet saints Hafiz and Rumi shared their divine revelations in the form of poetry and prose through the oral tradition of parables, koans and stories.

Jnaneshwar's *Bhagavad-Gita,* the *Holy Bible,* and the *Kabala* are such manuscripts. The teachings of the *Vedas,* the *Upanishads, The Yoga Sutras, The Tibetan Book of Living and Dying* and others, were all written to help human beings understand their essential nature.

The teaching, *"God is everywhere, most importantly in you,"* is the core message of all knowers of the truth around the world.

The poet saint Jelaluddin Rumi has been called the greatest mystic of Islam. He was born on September 30, 1207, and died in Southern Turkey, 1273. Andrew Harvey, author of *Teachings of Rumi*, tells us, "Everything Rumi wrote or transmitted has the unmistakable authority of total inner experience, the authority of a human being who has risked and given everything to the search for divine Truth."

> What we have to do is to become the Sun itself,
> So all fear of separation can forever be ended.
>
> —Rumi

Legend has it that the poet saint Kabir lived one hundred-twenty years, possibly from 1398-1518 AD. In 1604, *Songs of Kabir* became part of the Sikh holy book, *The Adi Grant*, located now in the Golden Temple in Amristsar, India.

Kabir referred to himself as a Muslim weaver, but Muslim weavers of the time were steeped in a combination of teachings including Hindu, low Buddhist, and the Tantric teachings of the Naths.

> Allah is hidden
> In each body.
> Think about it.
> He is the same
> Both in Hindus and Turks
> This is what Kabir

Is shouting out
So loudly.

-Kabir
Raga Asa

Fifteen lunar days;
Seven weekdays,
Kabir says, "They have neither
A bank on this side,
Nor a bank on that side."
Sages and saints learn the secret:
The Creator, Deva, is everywhere

-Kabir
"*Sloka*" from *Raga Gauri*

He is very near—
Right in your own heart
Why do you leave Him and wander
far away?
He for whom you searched the world Over.
Is so very near.

-Kabir
Raga Gauri

Rabbi Israel Baal Shem Tov was born over three hundred years ago. He made it possible for everyone in his community, from peasant to scholar, to know the inner dimensions of the Torah, the mystical teachings of Judaism.

> "Deveikut implies constant communion with God, a vivid and overwhelming consciousness of the Omnipresent as the sole true reality."
>
> —Rabbi Israel
> *Baal Shem Tov*

Tukaram, affectionately called "Tuka," was said to have lived from 1608-1649 near the village of Dehu, India. He was an ascetic who made God so central in his thought that he lost all interest in his body. He did not believe that a person needed to be a monk in order to be spiritually evolved. He taught that each man has his own duties and needs to be responsible for them.

> This whole universe,
> everything included,
> consists of one substance.
>
> -Tukaram

Meeting My First Saint

When I was in my early thirties, one of my teachers was on a search for a "true Guru." He wanted his own students to meet a saint, an enlightened being, and while in India discovered the great saint Swami Muktananda. In 1974 my teacher rented a giant concert hall and introduced this great being to his own students and to the people of San Francisco.

As a child I had heard about the powers of the saints, but I didn't know that saints exist in every culture and in every spiritual tradition on earth. After my initial introduction to Swami Muktananda, my natural curiosity brought me to an evening program to meet him in person.

In a question-and-answer period that night, I remember seeing a man in the audience stand up and ask Swami Muktananda, "If you can heal a person with diabetes or cancer, why don't you?"

I remember Muktananda saying that it was not his job. His job was to heal our understanding.

What did he mean by "heal our understanding"?

Over the next two decades I discovered the part of his message I felt was personally meant for me. Inside myself I heard him say, "Carol, transform the beliefs, concepts, habits and family programming that are obstacles to experiencing the truth of who you really are."

Muktananda was one of the rare saints born to give us the experience of our own true identity. Through decades of selfless service, study, and meditation he had earned the power to give "Shaktipat," the awakening in students of their dormant spiritual Kundalini energy. Through Shaktipat, he initiated the ongoing process of inner purification in thousands of seekers around the world.

Muktananda was an empathetic and generous teacher, but he also demanded rigorous discipline of serious students. He taught us that yoga means "union with God," and that it was the goal of his teachings to offer true seekers the experience of God within themselves, and to help each attain the divine state of steady union as God.

Muktananda's simple, sparkling clarity made it easy for me to understand the teachings of other saints and spiritual traditions. He was my inspiration for writing *Beginning Saint*—the unfolding process of evolving the saint that already exists within us.

Saints Have All the Fun

I've always loved and admired people who have a sense of humor. I've tried to analyze what it is about how they think that makes them so funny and causes them to have so much fun.

It's their perceptions! They are not stuck in any one viewpoint. They have the wonderful freedom to take all kinds of perspectives.

A comedian, like the poet, painter, and musician, can transport us momentarily to a completely different reality.

Great beings, too, have lots of fun. They rise above negative emotions, painful feelings, and small ideas. They unhook us from stuck points of view and keep us and themselves firmly on the path of love and light.

When you focus your mind on a great saint—*a being of light*—you, too, transcend limited states of mind. You feel merged with the energy of the saint. The source of this phenomenon is the vibration of such a being.

There are stories of people who went to visit the great saint Bhagawan Nityananda of India. "Bade Baba," as they called him, rarely spoke a word, but in his presence many people found their whole life changed. There are many reports of healings that took place around him without a word being spoken by anyone.

At other times he would give succinct lessons. On the subject of grace, he taught that *grace provides the shortest route and fastest way home to the place of our origin with the Infinite.*

Students of the Catholic Saint Padre Pio reported seeing him for the first time in their dreams. He would give them some advice, and later when they met him in person, he would question them to see if they had done what he asked.

There is a saying, *"It takes one to know one."* When you recognize greatness, it is because there is greatness inside you that resonates with the other person's light. It is a sign that you already have many of the same qualities within you.

Recall a person you completely admire. As you think of them, feel how their light and energy fuses with your own. All separation between you disappears and you experience being *one* with them.

How Saints Teach

Saints teach with every encounter. Whenever I met with one favorite saint, she would laugh and play with me. I felt so close to her, so natural and happy to be in her presence.

One day when I happened to speak directly with her, she tickled me and playfully hit me with her wand of peacock feathers.

In return I playfully tapped her knee. She was not at all concerned that I had touched her in that way.

After I walked away from her, however, I realized I had actually "hit her" and I immediately withdrew from her in shame. I told myself, "Carol, you should never hit anyone, let alone a saint. How awful you are!"

The next time I walked up to greet her I was very quiet and withdrawn in guilt, feeling I had done something really terrible. I couldn't look her in the eye.

She looked at me directly and said, "Playing humble, are you?"

I realized in that moment that she was not admonishing me for my playfulness and license, but giving me a great lesson about trusting my own inner self—my inner spontaneity, as well as hers.

In subsequent talks she reminded her students that if we want to relinquish our egos, we should let go of punishing ourselves.

In another experience with a saint I learned a lesson in trust. A monk asked my husband if he would take the saint's glasses home with us to be repaired. My husband happily said "yes," wrapped them carefully, and packed them in his suitcase.

We boarded the plane and took off on a beautiful sunny day. However, within the hour, and two thousand miles from home, the captain came on the loudspeaker and said, "I have some good news and some bad news. The good news is that the Steelers have just won the Super Bowl. The bad news is we have just lost an engine."

I immediately started shaking a million miles an hour. My husband looked over at me and said, "Why are you shaking so much?" Then, laughing, he reminded me, "Carol, why would an enlightened being send his glasses back on a plane that wasn't going to get there?"

Saints have generous hearts and are encouraging. In the company of a saint you always feel loved (unless your own mind is busy evaluating yourself like mine was). Saints are uninterested in how others judge them.

One saint told his student, "I don't care if you love me or hate me. That's of no concern to me. If you dislike me intensely, however, you won't be able to get me out of your mind. Then I can show you how truly great you are and how much you are really loved."

Saints engage in creating a culture of love for everyone. Saints want everyone to feel the intense happiness they know is possible. They know, that as your understanding grows, so too does your love for yourself, others, and life. They know that all riches, ecstasy, and peace automatically follow from the continual application of universal Truth. They know that living in joy and abundance is the natural state of your God-Self.

Saints are aware that each person is doing his best at the level of his awareness, but they also know that forgetting the truth is a cause of both physical and emotional pain.

The Saint in You

Since you have already managed the most important task—being born into a human body—you have already signed up for this evolutionary process.

If you wish, however, you can speed up the process for the sheer joy of it!

Your primary challenge is to become conscious of your natural inner characteristics, powers, and abilities. It requires reminding yourself that your essential nature is divine, and to continually realign and attune your mind and behavior from the awareness of your God-Self at all times. It is the most important challenge of any lifetime.

You are a spiritual being already. You are made of the same stuff, the same energy that makes up the entire universe. You're made of energy so subtle there are no instruments designed (so far) to measure it. What does this mean for you and me?

It means that each person embodies much more power than he or she currently can conceive of.

It means that when humans recognize that God exists in everyone, most importantly in their own selves, they will naturally be compelled to treat themselves and each other with much more love, respect, and care.

See God in Yourself

Exercise 2

Please take a few moments to do the following exercise:

1. Find a comfortable place to sit, in either a cross-legged position or on a straight-backed chair with your feet flat on the floor.
2. Place your hands in your lap or on your thighs.
3. Take a long breath in and a long breath out while relaxing your body. Repeat this several times.
4. Close your eyes. Feel your body and mind quieting.
5. Place your attention on your body while breathing slowly in and out.

Say to yourself:

God is in my feet, my legs, my lower body.
God is in my abdomen, my stomach, my back and my chest.
God is in my heart and lungs.
God is in my shoulders, my arms and hands.
God is in my neck, in my face, my brain, my eyes, ears, nose and throat.
God surrounds my body.
God is "in here" and "out there."
God is looking from these eyes.
God is the love I am.
God is the life I am.

6. Continue to breathe slowly and smoothly. Now close your eyes for a few moments while you experience the feeling of God's Presence within you.
7. Notice the peaceful physical sensations in your body. What do you feel?

Practice Seeing God in Others

Exercise 3

Bring your attention to your body for a few moments.

1. Relax your head, neck and shoulders.
2. Notice your chest and stomach muscles.
3. Slowly take in a long and deep breath and exhale slowly while relaxing even more deeply.
4. Continue to relax your body.
5. Now, look around the room and begin to notice each object in the room from the following perspective:

   I see you, God, in the form of the light coming in the window.
   I see you in the people on the sidewalk.
   I see you in the painting on the wall.
   I hear you in the clinking of dishes, the dogs barking next door and the water flowing from the faucet.
   I recognize you in the people on their way to work.
   I see you in the form of my town, state, country and the Earth.

God is everywhere is the underlying message of *The Golden Rule: "Do unto others as you would have others do unto you,"* and *The Bill of Rights: "We hold these truths to be self-evident, that all men are created equal."* God has manifested as millions of human beings, experiencing millions of individual lives.

Each of us embodies the arms, legs, mind and heart of God.

Experiencing God in Your Body

Exercise 4

Take in a slow, even breath, hold it for a moment, then exhale slowly and long.

1. Relax your head, neck, shoulders, chest, abdomen and legs.
2. Now read the following statements to yourself:

   God lives within me and creates through me.
   I am God, living and loving in the world.
   I am God, totally present in each of my life tasks.
   I am God supporting me through life.
   I am God loving me through my body.
   My body is the body of God.
   My breath is the breath of God.
   My mind is the mind of God.
   My heart is the heart of God.
   God is present in every point in space.

3. Feel the bliss of this recognition. As you continue with your day, notice the sweet feelings that linger.

Tai-an asked Po-Chang, "I have been seeking for the Buddha, but do not yet know how to go on with my research."

Po-chang replied, "It is very much like looking for an ox when you are riding on one."

—Po-Chang

Chapter 4

How to Recognize God

Jessica

A pre-school teacher passed out paper and crayons to a whole class full of three- and four-year olds. Over on the other side of the room was Jessica, a little girl diligently working on her drawing.

The teacher decided to check out how Jessica was doing, so she walked over to her and asked, "Jessica, what are you drawing?"

Jessica replied, "I'm drawing a picture of God." The teacher said, "But Jessica, nobody knows what God looks like."

Jessica replied, "Just give me a minute and they will."

—Recalled by Leo, a friend

You'll Know Me by Your Feelings

You can often "hear" God by listening to your feelings. Notice what you feel inside when you focus your love, whether on yourself, another person, nature, music, an animal, or a particular place or event.

Notice how wonderful you feel.

If it weren't for this exquisite, splendid ability—the ability to love, would anyone choose to play the game of life? Would a mother care for her child? Would a young man marry? Would a child hug a puppy?

Human love is the path both to experiencing and to knowing God. When we give and receive love with no expectations, we are God in action.

Ultimately, everything human beings do is for love. Men and women sacrifice their lives for the love of an idea, for the love of their country, their children, their concept of God, and for their desire to make a difference in the world.

Our species is "crazy for love." We love to work, to contribute to others, and to support our families. We study for the love of knowledge, for the love of games and for understanding. We teach and help others for the love of each other, for the love of common understanding, for the love of action, for the love of drama, play, beauty and order.

We love to love.

Because God is everywhere, and God's most important quality is love, love, too, exists in infinite forms.

Count the number of ways you experience love in your own life, and know that when you experience love in any of its forms, you are experiencing God. Say to yourself, "God is the love that I am."

When we feel love, it often feels generated by our physical heart. The great saint, Bhagawan Nityananda taught:

The Heart is the hub of all sacred places.
Go there and roam.

—Nitya Sutras

God exists in matter, energy, space and time ... and beyond.

Notice that sometimes God shows up in life as beauty and order, but other times in what might appear to be chaos or disorder.

Yet even in those times of seeming chaos or disorder, when we look from God's eyes, we see perfection, we see the relatedness of all things, and we see the exquisite beauty of the whole amazing spectrum of forms and functions. We see the fabulous cast of characters in our life's play.

When we look from our hearts we are the witness to the most captivating and penetrating dramas imaginable. What an amazing life we live!

God Is Right Where You Are

In the same way that you feel the energy of a saint when you think of him or her, you can feel the love and energy of God existing in all forms. When you first begin to feel this, it may take a bit of practice before becoming second nature.

When you, for instance, see a beautiful tree, you'll know that its essence is God. It may be called a "magnolia," an "oak," an "aspen" or a "eucalyptus," but with practice you'll come to know that its true identity is God.

In the very same way, you'll start to recognize the God-Self in each of your family members, your friends, and your co-workers.

How do we know we're experiencing God?

Each of us has experienced innumerable instances of divine energy coursing through our veins, but may not have recognized these experiences as manifestations of God.

Sometimes we believe that only "good" experiences are God, and that the thoughts, feelings and experiences we interpret as less than desirable are not God.

But that is not true.

We choose how to interpret our experiences. We decide to see something as something to be agitated about or as something to feel uplifted by. It is all up to us.

Eventually we come to see that everything that happens in our lives is a gift for our benefit. We come to know that God exists in infinite forms and that identifying ourselves as God is not a boastful thing to do. It is the Truth.

Say to yourself, "God is the love that I am."

As you experience each attribute of God as your very own, it will be easier for you to trust your God-Self.

Building the conviction that "God is the love that I am" is the task of the beginning saint. Practicing your power and activating your creativity will, over time, free your greatness—and reveal and accomplish your life's purpose.

Through the simple exercises you have performed already, you've had at least three experiences of God:

You have experienced God as you, living in your body;

You have experienced God in others; and

You have experienced God existing in animate and inanimate objects.

Your spiritual momentum will increase as you continue to remind yourself of God existing in all these forms and beyond.

Smoggy Days

I grew up in Los Angeles when it was impossible to see through the smog to the other side of the street. On those days I had to reassure myself that the other side of the street actually existed. The beautiful San Bernardino Mountains were obscured and the starry skies, too. I had to remind myself that they really were there.

I love to fly. I always sit next to the window. From that vantage point everything makes more sense. Because I've had the experience of flying above the clouds, I know that the sun always shines up there.

Remembering that the sun exists allows me to let go of feeling too moody on overcast days. Because I've experienced the sun bright and warm somewhere above me, I know it is there, even if I can't fly to it. New Yorkers have difficulty seeing the starry nights, too, because of the abundance of city lights, but those living in the Rocky Mountains, the High Sierras, or Hawaii, know what stars are all about—they know that even shooting stars exist. They have had an experience of the infinite universe.

It's the same with God. We may have heard about God. Others talk about God, but until we've had an "*Aha*" moment of actually feeling God in our life, we might not realize that God is right where we are. It's very easy for each of us to get so caught up in our habitual ways of seeing that we forget that God also exists in everyday things.

My friend Dina says that we tend to relate to God as if God were Santa Claus, believing the words in the Christmas song by Haven Gillespie and J. Fred Coots: "*You better watch out, you better not cry, you better not pout, I'm a-tellin' you why—Santa Claus is coming to town. He knows when you are sleeping, he knows when you're awake. He knows if you've been bad or good ... so be good for goodness sake!"*

Many western traditions have taught that God exists everywhere, but outside the individual—often blaming or rewarding people for their behavior and attitudes. They've taught that God is punishing more often than loving—that God is a force to fear more than a force to embrace and trust.

Eastern traditions give names to the various functions of God's powers. In India, the power of beauty and abundance is symbolized by a form of God called *Goddess Lakshmi.* In Chinese philosophy, the same powers of God are symbolized by *Goddess Kuan Yin.* Hindus name the creative and courageous aspect of God *Shiva.* In the West, we emphasize similar specific powers of God when we refer to God as *Cosmic Consciousness, Divine Energy,* or even as *Mother Nature.*

Each of us has multitudinous experiences of God daily, but may not have recognized these experiences *as* God. We may not have known that what we were seeing, hearing, feeling, tasting, touching and knowing were God's infinite eternal forms.

How many of us find God in challenges, hard work, pain, loss? How many of us see God in learning, struggle, and determination? How many of us recognize God existing in our frustration?

As you proceed on your path, you will learn to recognize that struggle and suffering are also vehicles for growth and transformation.

As a beginning saint, you will become ever more adept at sifting the true from the false, the light from the darkness.

The sifting will begin and continue until you realize your own perfection and until all your God-Self powers and attributes come into full bloom.

See God in the Body

When you honor your body and take care of it, it treats you well. The body contributes to your spiritual liberation. It is the temple in which you experience yourself as God. When you treat your body as your trusted friend, it helps you to know and experience your God-Self.

Your body is your most sensitive meter for recognizing God and God's love within. That is why many saints teach that having a human body is essential to the evolution of the soul. It gives you immediate feedback about the mental and emotional direction in which you are going. All your thoughts and feelings are great communications to you from God within you. You can use your senses. Your body is a perfect, physical vehicle of God. Through your body God experiences self-awareness, pleasure, and pain. It is a form God takes in order to play this glorious game of life.

The saints remind us that to earn a human body is a very great accomplishment. They tell us, "Respect your human body, because God lives and has His being within it."

Through your senses you notice how you feel and what you need to work on. If you feel upset, God within is telling you that a correction in your perception is needed (if you want to feel better). If I'm acting grumpy and feeling out of sorts with my mate or my friend, I know I'm not attuned to the highest truth of either one of us. If I'm feeling sick to my stomach or feeling pressure in my head, it's a clue for me that I have either gone into agreement with a lie, gone into doubt about myself, or haven't been listening to God in my body. I know I have some more work to do on myself.

The saints remind us that when we learn to listen to the *"still small voice"* of our God-Self, we can know what God knows, feel God's presence everywhere, and experience the power of God's unlimited wisdom, creativity and love.

As a therapist, my job is to help people identify the thoughts and assumptions that are at the core of their discomfort, and to help them rewrite their "scripts." If they are feeling happy and content, God shows up as a delicious experience of peace and well-being. The line of communication is pretty simple. However, if they're not aware of God's Presence, and they don't know that God is always communicating with them, they may have misinterpreted what they feel.

For each of us, the major challenge is to listen and accurately differentiate the messages of our limited self or ego from the messages of our omniscient God-Self.

Feel the Presence of God in Music

When I was a child growing up in Los Angeles, I lived two blocks from the Leimert Park Movie Theater. Almost every Saturday my mother would give my siblings and me a quarter each for the double matinee, along with a box each of Jujubes and Malt Balls.

I will feel forever grateful for growing up with musical comedies. For the most part their melodies and lyrics were about "*whistling a happy tune,*" rather than about pain and suffering. They were playful, positive and joyful.

Musical teams such as Rogers and Hammerstein, Lerner and Lowe, and the Gershwins were the princes of music. They composed songs entitled: *If I Loved You*, *It Must Be Love*, *Somewhere Over the Rainbow*, *Happy Talk*, and *Singin' in the Rain*, all of which ignited in me feelings of peace, love, joy, and creativity … the qualities of the God-Self.

In Hollywood they called it "magic." Even though movies are fantasy, the vibrations created by their music are real. I felt cellular effects in my body that I can feel to this day.

I had no words to explain what was happening to me. I was ecstatic—absorbed in the feelings engendered by the music, the expressions of love, and the happy lyrics. After attending each musical performance I'd feel so filled with love, so excited, and experiencing so much joy inside that I'd dance all the way home. For hours afterward nothing could penetrate my delight and bliss. Often I'd be humming or singing the songs for days on end.

I learned that I could feel the same wonderful feelings of love, freedom, and sweetness by singing to myself whenever I wanted. Today I know that my absorption in sound is a form of "*practicing the presence of God*."

As you go about your own day, notice which melodies resonate with your own inner pulses. Notice which beats, which vibrations, push you to dance. Notice the joyful feeling of a thought-free mind that comes with nearly all music.

In the same way that music provides a refuge from the mind, you may experience similar feelings of peace or bliss or joy in many other ways. Perhaps your sensitivity to nature, to fragrances, or to touch, ignites such feelings in you.

Notice when you experience them and discover how to return to those great, blissful states whenever you choose.

Hear and Feel God in Laughter

Neither my mother, my grandmother, nor my husband, Bruce, is a particularly good storyteller, but if they see something in life that's funny to them, they absolutely can't stop laughing. No one anywhere near them can stop laughing either.

Maybe you know people like that. Maybe you are one of them. The music and beat of their laughter is so intoxicating! If they happen to be in an auditorium with thousands of people and they start laughing, soon the entire building is roaring and people are clutching their ribs.

If God is in everything, then God definitely exists in our laughter. Have you ever found yourself feeling better after a good laugh? Laughter is cleansing and releases tension. How many times have you felt anxious, serious and uncomfortable—then all of a sudden something tickles you?

The impulse of laughter creates endorphins in the body,and emotionally transports you to another reality. A chemical change and shift in energy happens in your body when you laugh. Laughter is the very best medicine.

When Norman Cousins, editor and tireless advocate for world peace, learned that he was terminally ill, he shared with his family and friends, "If what I think and do in my life has made me sick, perhaps if I do just the opposite I could heal my self."

He asked his family members and friends to bring him comedies, jokes, poems, stories—anything that could make him laugh.

Cousins moved himself from the hospital to a hotel, bought himself a movie projector so he could watch the Marx Brothers and other comedies, and miraculously recovered. He concluded that he had literally *laughed himself well*, and wrote about it. His experiments on himself helped doctors to recognize that when the body's endorphins are mobilized through love, happiness, and laughter, the body's immune system can also be regenerated.

Feel God in Silence

God exists in silence, whole and perfect, containing all limitless dimensions of creation, all potentials and possibilities, all universes, all consciousness, all action and non-action, all order and all chaos … all space, void, energy, and beyond … infinitely.

When you quiet your mind, you can feel silence bursting with consciousness—an alive, pulsing, thought-free state. When you practice being in silence, you experience your peaceful, whole, essential God-Self with *"no pictures or conversations."* Your limited ideas fall away. You allow yourself the invisible ecstasy of melding with cosmic consciousness. You let go of the small self. Your awareness expands, and you recognize you've never really been alone or separate from God.

You feel absolutely stopped in silence, yet the humming of consciousness underlies everything.

When my grandmother said to me, "I can't die now. I don't know where I'm supposed to go," both of us were absolutely stopped in silence, consciously faced with the enormity of the unknown. Neither of us knew what might come next. We each experienced the abrupt death of past concepts, and, at that moment, *hit the wall* of our limited understanding.

Like everyone who faces death, we each had to surrender our known worlds and trust the silence, knowing our larger God-Self exists perfectly there too.

God Exists in Perfect Timing

When you place an order for something with God, and trust that it will be forthcoming, you often receive much more than you ever counted on.

Newlyweds George and Kathy wanted more than anything to live and raise their children in Santa Fe, the town where they grew up. Even though each had a good job, they agreed there was no way they could afford to buy a house in their old neighborhood. They decided on a house in a less expensive area twenty miles away where they could have a bigger living room and kitchen and a yard for their animals.

During the next six months it became very clear that it didn't matter how big or fancy their house was, what they really valued most was living close to their families and friends. They each independently asked their higher self for a "more-workable solution."

One day, while scanning the real estate section of the local paper, Kathy saw an ad that read, "Desperately need to trade our house for yours no matter the size. We need to be closer to work."

Kathy called the owners and discovered the house was only six blocks from her parents' home. Within a month she and George had officially traded houses with the other couple. They moved back to Santa Fe feeling completely grateful, astonished at the sequence of events, and with new appreciation for *the ways God listens.*

Kathy told me, *"We're learning to trust in that unseen energy existing everywhere."*

When I saw them last, they were excitedly planning for the birth of their first child.

God Exists in All Seasons of Life

God's energy is ever-flowing and ever-changing. It's easy to see God in a newborn baby, but sometimes it is harder to see God in a grown man or a frail old woman on her deathbed.

As you practice seeing God everywhere, recognize God in every season, in every age, in every condition and in every situation. God's omnipotent powers are responsible for creation, for maintaining creation, and for dissolving creation.

You may have observed God existing in an exquisite ice crystal that, moments later, began melting, forming water droplets, and later still took the form of a pool of water.

The Basic Elements of Life

There are three basic powers and characteristics of God. Just for fun we'll call them "the three omnis." They include: omnipresence, the only and all-encompassing God Presence that exists everywhere; omniscience, the power of God that knows everything; and omnipotence, God's unlimited power to create, maintain, and dissolve creations.

Since these are characteristics of God, and "what is true of the ocean is true of the drop," we learn that we embody the same powers. Many of us, however, have little awareness of what it means that these powers and abilities exist within us. We do not truly comprehend the possibilities of our own omnipresence, omniscience, or omnipotence. We have absolutely no idea how to use these indwelling powers and are unaware of the great, unlimited potentials we could fulfill.

But as we explore and practice using these powers, they become more visible and accessible to us. We discover that each power has infinite facets and dimensions.

Operating Procedures

Ultimately, what each of us experiences in our life is dependent on our individual understanding and on the choices we make. That is why it is so essential that we learn how to consciously apply our powers and how to create the best for ourselves and the world.

Our *free will* is the steering device that allows us to operate our lives. Our individual free will—our ability to choose—enables us to consciously use our minds to create the lives we want. Through our *free will* we can learn how to manifest our dreams.

Nothing is either right or wrong in the universe, but over lifetimes human beings have formulated societal rules that have allowed members of societies to co-exist and to survive more successfully. The saints tell us there is actually an overriding tendency towards good operating in the universe.

Our beliefs and values, however, have influenced how we have used our *free will* in the past. Those beliefs continue to influence how life unfolds for us until we consciously intervene and create new choices. We find that we're able to use them, to the degree that we come to understand our powers, trust that they exist, and apply them in our lives.

Through the choices we make, we create consequences in every second of our lives—some we are aware of, but most we are not aware of.

That is why the thoughts we think have so much power. They form the impressions that shape the moment-to-moment direction of those three powers we embody.

Omnipresence

God Is Everywhere

The first omni, *omnipresence,* is the core essential and ancient teaching of enlightened saints: *God is everywhere.* Any thought that limits us from knowing or seeing God's presence everywhere, especially within ourselves, is out of sync with Universal Truth. Limited thoughts and the feelings these generate show up in both the physical and feeling world we live in, and unfold in both our individual and collective lives.

Knowledge of God's omnipresence tells us that the *Creator of All Universes* exists within all emotional and psychological states, all attitudes, all channels, all dimensions, all frequencies, all waves, and beyond. Realizing this to be so, we ask, "So how do I know if I'm evolving toward God or away from God?

Conscious awareness of your own thinking and feeling state is essential. Your thoughts let you know whether or not you are telling the highest truth. Your feelings help you know whether you're aligned with your radiant, awake God-Self, or are in a doubting, cloudy, "small-self" state.

Just as you can tell when you are feeling healthy, strong, happy, safe, content, peaceful and joyful, you can also feel when something's "off." When you feel agitated or confused, when your awareness seems clouded, or even when your feelings manifest as an anxious or queasy stomach—these are signs that your perceptions need "window washing."

Although God is equally present within you both in light—when you're awake in the state of your radiant God-Self, and in darkness—when you're in a depressed, doubting, "small-self" state, in this direction or that direction, it's usually easier to function when you can see your way and both your mind and body are uncluttered by obstacles.

For a beginning saint, evolving means first being aware of what and how you are feeling, and then realizing that all your feelings are gifts that can help you grow. Great teachers exist in all cultures, to help coach students how to clear their minds of mistaken beliefs and attitudes.

It's up to you, however, to know where the advice and teachings are coming from and to notice for yourself if your teacher is emulating his or her own teachings. That's why it's important to find the wisest person to learn from.

How do you feel in his presence? Do her words uplift and ring true to you inside? Does he appear to be established in his own teaching? Has she attained peace of mind, equality consciousness and lightheartedness as far as you know?

God Is Omnipresent

Exercise 5

The first omni

1. What do you feel when you:
   Think of someone you admire?
   When you believe you've done a good job?
   When you see a beautiful tree?
   When you think of someone you love?
   When you hear an uplifting song?
   When you think of a good friend?
   When you experience the touch of a loved one?
   When you love someone or something?
2. What physical sensations do you have when you are peaceful?
3. Every few minutes throughout the day, notice where you are. Find a way to appreciate the location and/or your emotional state at the time.

4. Choose something you like about your life at this moment.
5. Notice what you feel inside when you think a happy thought.

How Do I Use My Power of Omnipresence?

Notice what conversations you've been having with yourself. What beliefs, expectations or ideas have contributed to what you are experiencing?

God is synonymous with love, so when you are feeling love inside, your mind and body register, "I like this feeling," and you automatically feel the Presence of God within you.

This doesn't mean that God is not there when you feel agitated or depressed, but you are less likely to feel the unlimited *clear-sky* qualities of God at such times.

If life is coming through fuzzy, you know it's time to replace the batteries—or in this case your thoughts—so that you can feel your highest God-Self perfectly.

At such times, ask yourself, *"What thought am I thinking?* How does that thought make me feel inside?

If you don't like the thought, then say to yourself, "I let go of all thoughts and feelings unlike my highest God-Self."

When you feel you've dropped the thought and regained your focus, ask yourself, *"What thoughts could I think that would make me feel better inside?"*

And, there you go ... don't you feel better already? (The thought might even be an angry thought, but at the moment you say it, you've released it from your mind and it's gone. Storing up hurtful thoughts inside can be even more destructive than acknowledging to yourself what you are feeling.)

When you replace those hurtful or limiting thoughts with more positive messages, you start to feel even more in control of your life, healthier and happier. When you get *foggy thoughts* out of the way, you automatically return to your naturally joyful state.

One aspect of omnipresence is knowing that God, and all God's attributes, are totally within your spirit, mind and body.

Omniscience

God Is All-Knowing

Your God-Self Knows Everything About Everything

The second omni: Within God's power of omniscience lies the most important power for living life as a human being. Some call it the *Universal Mind* or the *Mind of God.*

Each of us has an individual mind connected to, and inseparable from, the one, all-encompassing, *Universal Mind.* Our omniscience and intuition are powers functioning through this all-knowing power of God. It acts like a non-judgmental mirror, simply reflecting back to us what we think or feel into it.

If I am thinking, *"Oh, what a beautiful day it is—I'm so grateful to be alive,"* the Universal Mind mirrors back corresponding thoughts and feelings, which in turn create physical effects in my body. My body responds to the images with warmth and love, and both my physical heart and emotional heart feel happy, too.

Our power to know is directly related to our ability to tap into the *Universal Mind*: But if I think a fearful thought such as

"I wonder if I'll be able to pay my bills this month?" the *Universal Mind* also reflects back my thinking, in physical tension, anxiety, and worry. This thinking has the effect of increasing my heart rate and adrenalin flow, creating lines on my face, and causing feelings of irritation in my body. My ability to use the Universal Mind is directly related to the level of my consciousness.

The power to know is a basic attribute of the *Universal Mind,* but without the awareness that we can *"just know things,"* we may create scary thoughts that obscure true knowledge from ourselves. Our capacity to know and understand is limited only by our level of awareness and by our judgments, beliefs, desires, and choices.

Go Home, Annie

Practicing Her Intuition

Annie was on her way to a meeting when an inner-knowing message surfaced in her mind, "Go home." She was not feeling afraid of anything at the time, nor was she avoiding the meeting, nor was she ill. But she listened to the message and drove home anyway.

When she arrived, she discovered that a water main had broken on the second floor of her house and water was gushing out of the ceiling onto the first floor. She immediately received another inner message, "Turn off the water valve." The fire department came within minutes and she was able to save nearly everything in her house.

You may have had similar experiences in your own life. It's important, however, that you differentiate an authentic message from an anxious thought.

Inner knowing doesn't scare you. It usually comes in the form of a firm but clear statement or feeling—a feeling that says, "yes," if it's true, and "no," if it's not true, or even, "this part is accurate and that part is not." The ability to quickly validate messages comes with practice.

The Power of Intuition

Your five senses give you information about the world, but it's up to you to develop your ability—the intuitive wisdom we all have—to recognize the highest truth. The omniscient power of God is also known as *Divine Consciousness, God Consciousness* or *Universal Mind*, and is the ability that lies within each of us to access unlimited knowledge.

I.Q. tests assess a person's *limited knowledge*. Omniscience is our God-Self's *unlimited power to know.* It manifests in a variety of ways. Sometimes we know something intellectually because we've thought it through and it makes sense.

The higher type of knowing—intuition—is beyond thinking and beyond the intellect. It is God's knowing within us.

The sages tell us that, because God is within us, each of us has access to infinite knowledge. Practices such as self-inquiry, visualization and meditation (quieting the mind) help us access that inner wisdom. Our five senses give us information about the world, but it's up to us to turn to and develop the wisdom of our intuition in order to recognize the highest truth.

My friends who are musicians demonstrate this all the time. Many never learned to read notes, yet they have no problem feeling and transmitting their inner rhythms and their own inner compositions. They access their music in a state of meditation, immersed in vibrations that lie beyond the individual mind.

Visual artists—painters, sculptors, photographers, architects and designers of all kinds—are sensitive to sending and receiving knowledge through intuitive channels.

Most great scientists, sages, poets and artists show great respect for natural knowing. Having highly developed access to their inner-knowing, they are often seen as prophets, psychics or saints. By tapping into the Universal Mind, they express the infinite forms of God's wisdom, intelligence, and beauty.

Your own intuition is an aspect of your omniscience, and is an essential tool for verifying higher truths.

Accessing Your Intuition Through Meditation

Experiencing the practice of meditation—quieting your thoughts at will—shows you that the intellect alone is not enough to propel you through the mire of the individual mind. It shows you how important *Practicing the Presence of God* is to breaking through the limitations of the material world.

If you've already been introduced to the skill and practice of meditation, you know how essential meditation is to experiencing the thought-free state of God. When you learn to quiet your mind, you let go of ideas and beliefs about God and directly perceive God within yourself.

It's a kind of "sunbath"—through meditation you immerse yourself in light and learn to calm your mind and pay attention to the subtle feelings and awareness of your inner self. Immersed in meditation, you feel at one with your God-Self. In meditation, you easily access the source of your omniscience and intuition.

Meditation is a great gift. Learning to meditate is learning to *practice the presence of God*. (In Chapter 7 we will explore more about meditation in depth.)

Learning to recognize truth amidst non-truth is also an important element of your unfolding omniscience. How do you do that?

As a beginning saint you will find teachings that resonate with your God-Self. Some knowledge is self-evident—those teachings that simply feel true and make sense to you even when there is no external evidence of their truth. You will find yourself recognizing truths taught by enlightened beings because their teachings will resonate immediately with your own inner knowing—especially your heart.

As you hear or read a teaching of a great one, ask yourself, "Does this feel true to me inside? Does this perspective make ultimate sense to me? Can I apply it in my life? Do these understandings help me to feel happier, freer, and more at peace in the world? Do these understandings help me contribute my best to myself, my family, my community and my world?"

Have you ever had an experience of your intuition working perfectly and revealing important information or inner guidance? Maybe you rejected what your intuition told you, but later discovered it was correct all along. Each of us has access, but often we don't value it. We say to ourselves, "If it can't be confirmed through the intellect or scientific evidence, I'm not going to believe it."

The culture at large often doesn't value intuition, either. Up to now there have been no instruments available to measure the subtle energy of intuition; however, science and technology every day are moving towards being able to validate intuitive knowing.

Sages and saints, however, teach that true intuitive knowing is found in the evidence of your own experience. You discover that you have an *inner knowing meter* composed of both your body and your intellect. When both your inner awareness and the physical feelings in your body are aligned, you experience an undeniable certainty and power within.

As you practice reading your inner knowing, you soon realize your knowing is far superior to your everyday accumulation of information. You learn how to "check in" with your intuition and to guide your life from a state of trust.

You ask yourself questions like, "Does this feel accurate at the highest level of my awareness? When I consider this thought from its highest perspective, what does it register in my body?"

When no doubt or discrepancy arises between each answer, you can proceed with certainty.

You'll be able to discern the clarity of your intention in the same way. If you intend to create something in your life but your intention is wavering, it will also register on your *inner knowing meter* and affect the outcome.

A doubtful thought creates a feeling of doubt. On the other hand, a doubtful thought can also act as a friend, stating, "Let's get clearer about this before we proceed." Find out what the doubting thought is telling you.

Saints have richly developed internal instruments of higher awareness. They've practiced and refined their intuition through contemplation, self-inquiry, prayer and meditation. They know that God exists in their five senses, but also in other, less-developed senses. Saints have been able to experiment and explore facets of their God-Self inconceivable for the average person.

I remember visiting one saint who told me, *"In meditation you will discover there are unlimited worlds to explore, worlds far more beautiful, loving, and more interesting than this one."*

As you develop these more refined and sensitive channels of knowing, you, too, will begin to recognize expanded abilities. "Just knowing" frequently shows up as a direct here-and-now message, as in Annie's story when she heard, "Do this. This is correct. This message is for you. Go there!"

Trusting Your Omniscience

For centuries, scientists and sages have used their intentions, knowing, and prayers to facilitate healings, insight, and even scientific formulas.

Phil was such a guy. He was someone new to discovering his personal omniscience and thought he would try it out one night. He had been working on creating a healthy beverage that children could consume all day long without ill effects.

One night he decided to write his desire on a piece of notebook paper, place it on his nightstand, and see what happened in the morning. He wrote, *"Knowing God is everywhere, within everything and everyone, and knowing that my God-Self is merged with the intelligence and unlimited creativity of God, I know that a perfect formula for a healthy children's drink already exists in the unlimited possibilities of God and is revealing itself to me right now. I intend for this drink to add to the health and happiness of millions of adults and children around the world."*

Phil said that when he placed the note on his nightstand, his intuition told him he would get perfect results. Then he went to sleep.

In the morning he awoke to find numbers and letters scribbled on his tablet. *"Oh my God,"* he shouted. *"This is it!"*

He had no recollection of writing on the tablet during the night, but the "scribbling" was the exact formula for the new product he envisioned. It is currently being made and distributed throughout the United States and Great Britain.

Seeing God in Another

Doug learned of our concern over our friend John's future career choice. In response, Doug wrote back to us, *"I imagine John faces a real challenge. On the other hand, John is John and so only good things will continue to happen for him. His sails will eventually and gently catch a mighty gust of wind and the Lord will guide him to where he will be most happy, a place where his gifts will be nurtured and his life will be a grace to himself and others."*

Doug's knowing put our minds totally at ease. It was the knowing of a saint. It resonated with the truth of the God-Self that we know exists within everyone. *"The Lord,"* in this case, was John's own God-Self.

Doug was not only talking about John, he was talking about each one of us, knowing that because we are inseparable from God, we can't help but be a grace to ourselves and others. Our nature is to attract good things to ourselves.

As it happened, shortly after hearing from Doug, we noticed that John had become very clear about what he wanted to do in life and was investigating careers that provided a more perfect fit for him.

Seeing God in Every Issue, Situation, and Condition

Exercise 6

Beginning saints practice seeing God in every facet of life: every sound, smell, taste and touch; every problem, challenge, condition and relationship. They practice seeing every physical problem or event as an opportunity to grow.

Beginning saints look on challenges as good friends—helping expand their ability to use their inherent powers.

Review what happened already in your day today. Ask yourself:

1. What good could come out of what happened today?
2. What lesson could I take into tomorrow?
3. What is the gift in how I feel?
4. What's the teaching I am willing to hear?
5. Can I see the situation free of limitation?
6. How will seeing it that way help me?

God is Omnipotent—God Is All-Powerful

The third omni tells us that you have the power to create anything. There is nothing your God-Self cannot do. By simply tuning in to the potential of your own unlimited creativity, you become one with that power, embodying it within yourself.

When Jesus taught, ***"Ask, and it shall be given unto you,"*** he was telling you that a characteristic of your all-powerful God-

Self is your individual ability as an autonomous independent being to choose your life events.

This means that you have the power to direct your life, moment to moment, by what you choose to think and feel.

If you still live by a mental storehouse of old beliefs about what you *should* do, be, or have, it's time to let go of outdated ideas of limitation.

So, how do you do that?

You are the authority in your own life. Every instant of your life is determined to some extent by how you use your "free will." Each choice you make manifests … or doesn't … through the power of your conviction.

In the spiritual and cultural traditions in which we're raised, we're taught certain beliefs, rules, and expectations. Although we make conscious choices, we recognize that some of these come from limited understanding and may not be true for us now.

Perhaps you didn't realize you have the power to actually go for what you want. Many of us think we're not deserving or believe it isn't possible. Sometimes we think, *"those kinds of things—a great family, friends, money, or fame—belong to somebody else,"* and conclude, *"those kinds of things are impossible for me."*

In fact, it is our ability to choose that alone establishes our destiny.

Superstition and Bargaining

Brenda's brother Tommy was a roofer. While he was on a roof one afternoon he accidentally cut his leg. In two days his leg developed a serious staph infection. On seeing this, the doctor sent Tommy immediately to the hospital to try to save Tommy's life.

Brenda started bargaining with God. She pleaded, "Dear God, please save my little brother. I will suffer anything necessary for him. Give me all his pain. I've lived my life ... let him live instead of me. I can die now, just as long as he lives."

I asked Brenda if her prayers worked. "Oh yes," she said. "My brother recovered, but I'm still waiting for my own suffering to begin."

How many of us are still waiting for our suffering to start, perhaps as a result of a dirty deed we did, a consequence of some angry wish, or a superstitious belief that "we have to pay for it, whatever 'it' is"?

Brenda added, "I've had a hard time getting on with my own life plans, because I keep thinking I still have to pay for God saving Tommy's life."

Her mistaken understanding of God, superstition, and bargaining caused Brenda enormous suffering.

God doesn't work in the way that Brenda thought God did.

Sometimes when thoughts such as: "those kinds of good things only happen to rich people, or to those who have great families, friends, or fame"; or, "good things like that couldn't possibly happen to me," people feel they must bargain with God and do all kinds of other things, usually based on a superstition of one kind or another, to earn their desires.

What's really needed is living in the consciousness that everything you really want with all your heart is not only possible, but already exists in the quantum field getting ready to materialize in three-dimensional form.

Don't give up on your dreams or go into doubt about your ability to have, do, or be your dreams! Your God-Self is completely free and is connected to the unlimited, unconditional, abundance of the universe. It's here to support you.

All that is needed is to clearly define what you want and to expect that it is on its way: Like ordering from a menu, you are simply ordering it up. When you expect it to happen, your energy, thoughts and actions align with that expectancy.

If you had an opportunity to observe a true saint in action, you would know that a saint *never* bargains with God.

A saint does, however, show his or her appreciation and gratitude for God's gifts. Saints often thank God for gifts and prayers both before and after receiving them, because they trust God implicitly.

Assume the perspective: *"In the unlimited ethers of the universe, all possibilities already exist, and I am simply ordering up my rightful abundance."*

Know that your request happens in alignment with your thoughts and feelings, but also that you must be open to receiving it as well. That means trusting and recognizing that God is delivering your request in forms you may or may not recognize at first.

That's why it's so important to be clear about your order. God always delivers what you ask for, but if your request is unclear, you will receive unclear answers.

Since the God-Self who answers your prayers dwells within you, you need to apply your own self-effort.

You've heard the expression, *"It takes two wings to fly."* Your highest God-Self is holding up one wing, but your human self needs to hold up the other … with conviction, perseverance, and trust in the unseen.

If you've grown up unaware of the greatness that's possible for you, you may have to stretch your concept of what you can have, do, or be. Although you embody the freedom to create anything, there is the loving God-Self aspect of you that intends for everyone, including you, to win in life.

Since some of us have grown up believing there is not enough (success, food, candy, love, money) to go around, we find we have to let go of those old ideas of scarcity and know that *there is always enough.*

Note that power and responsibility go hand in hand, so in the process of placing your "order" it is wise to add, *"May this desire contain within it the highest benefit for everyone."*

You Are a Divine Creator

As a creator, you have an infinite palette of creativity, thoughts, feelings and abilities. You can create in multitudes of frequencies and vibrations—in one, two, three and more dimensions.

Musicians, writers, scientists, philosophers, teachers, sociologists, politicians, actors and filmmakers are people who like to create in the subtle realms. In the fields of sports, movement, and dance, people create in forms of action. Manufacturers, doctors, mechanics and all kinds of designers and technicians create in combinations of dimensions.

In the following exercise you are asked to create something you desire. When you consider it, understand that your desire could be to create a feeling such as happiness or peacefulness, a relationship such as intimacy and connectedness, a physical attribute such as bodily strength, or a financial condition such as abundant monetary resources.

Often in the West when someone asks us what we want, we immediately respond by thinking of a three-dimensional object we might like to have, like a new car. In the following exercise, see if you can expand your repertoire of creations to include feeling-states of playfulness, or peacefulness, or happiness.

God Is Omnipotent

Exercise 7

1. Name something you wish to happen, to have, or to feel.

   ____

2. Is there anything about this desire that you do not want?

   ____

3. State what you do want with no limitations. Include the feelings you would like to have.

   ____

4. State the desire in present time, as though it already exists.

   ____

5. When do you want this desire to show up in your life?

   ____

6. Thank your God-Self for creating it for you.

   ____

7. Feel it manifest as you describe it.

   ____

What did you experience in the process of creation? How could you apply this exercise the next time you create something?

Notice that the real shift happened in your own conscious awareness.

The Three Omnis in Your Own Life

Have you ever surprised yourself by simply thinking yourself somewhere and really feeling you were in that place, with full vision and awareness of what was happening? That is a mini-experience of your own omnipresence. The experience is the manifestation of just one of your inherent powers.

Have you ever been surprised by knowing something for no apparent reason? You just *knew* something was about to happen, but you had no idea how it was going to unfold? Then it did happen. That was an example of your omniscience.

Recall a time you felt your own power to make something happen. It may have been a physical healing of yourself or another. It may have been sending a thought message to a friend and their receiving it with confirmation. Or you *"very lightly"* wished something to happen, and moments later it did. That was an example of your omnipotence.

These are everyday examples of your omnipresence, omniscience and omnipotence.

The great ones tell us that these powers are available to everyone, but throughout history such powers were sometimes used in selfish ways.

The great teachers say that we can make our world even more splendid when we use our powers for good. They tell us that, although unlimited powers exist, it is how we apply these powers—the intention and feeling behind their use—that is all-important.

The Three Omnis

Exercise 8

Contemplate and answer the following questions:

1. How could you apply your power of omnipresence to help another person?

   ____

2. How could you use your power of omniscience to contribute to your community?

   ____

3. How could you use your omnipotence to benefit mankind?

   ____

Ye Shall Know the Truth
and the Truth Shall Set You Free

—John 8:32

Chapter 5

The Only Two Obstacles to Happiness

The enlightened saints of the East Indian scriptures, called *The Vedas*, tell us there are really only two obstacles to happiness. They are: 1) the belief you are separate from God, and 2) the choices you make.

The Belief You Are Separate from God

When you know God is everywhere, in everyone and in everything, you know it just isn't possible to be separate from God, because you *are* God.

An enlightened saint knows that *God is my very own Self.* His inner knowing helps him stand in the truth of his God-Self in every moment.

When a beginning saint practices this awareness, over time she, too, becomes anchored in this highest Truth.

When we feel small or are critical of ourselves or of one another, or when we minimize our abilities or dwell in depression, we feel separate from God. But when we make a choice to honor the best in us through our own free will, we experience happiness and a light heart.

The Choices You Make

Your choices become your lessons and teachers, and by contemplating them you acquire the understanding necessary to grow in consciousness—to become more aware of your inherent powers.

The Emperor's New Clothes

I'm reminded of the story of *The Emperor's New Clothes.* Remember how the emperor kept pretending he was wearing his new clothes, when actually he was completely naked? His subjects also were caught up in the lie, until one day a little boy shouted out, for everyone to hear, "*Why, the Emperor has no clothes!*"

In your own life, sometimes the exact opposite happens. You believe you are naked, when actually you are robed in riches beyond comprehension—clothed in the unlimited abundance of our own divinity.

As our thoughts create our reality, when we are angry, agitated, fearful, jealous, or having other limiting thoughts, we feel off-kilter and in pain. But this pain, like the Emperor's belief, is a delusion—caused by the belief that we are separate from God. We feel off-center because we are making choices that are not aligned with our true understanding and experience of God.

Doubt is also a formidable distracter. At times our inner intuition tells us we've made a choice aligned with truth, but later we doubt ourselves.

So, how do you maintain the truth and recognition of your abundant God-Self every day?

In moments where you forget your greatness, remind yourself to stay conscious—to be aware of the moments of impulsivity or reactivity when you tried to justify your behavior to yourself or others.

What is needed is to ask yourself, "What *do* I really want, instead?" And then make a new choice.

When you remind yourself of how the mind works, you realize that you can nip thoughts in the bud. You discover that you can catch a thought before it manifests, and let it go.

How? You learn to identify thoughts you want to keep—like memories of old friends—and also thoughts that no longer serve you.

Some people make a list of thoughts of truth they can refer to when they need to rebalance themselves. In this way they become the mechanics of their own finely tuned minds.

The ability to let go of a thought always exists in you, but sometimes you don't realize how simple it is to do so.

There's an old Chinese koan that asks, "How do you get a duck out of a bottle?" This question just stumps some people.

When I ask this question and the other person cannot think of an answer, I say, "Well, how did you get the duck into the bottle in the first place?

You simply thought it into the bottle … right?"

Only our own mind limits us. When we know that it's possible for us to just "drop or change a thought," we begin to know the enormous innate power we have. Our free will—our power—is in our own hands.

It's Up to You—a Ground Rule of God's Play

Let's review again the dynamic of *free will.*

When this glorious game of life was created, it came with opportunities to choose. What fun would the game be if we all felt that some unseen, some unknown force was always in charge and we didn't have any control over it? How would we feel if every move of the game and even the winner of the game were already determined? How many of us would want to play at all, in that case?

So, God, being the *Divine Gamester,* created the concept of *free will* and empowered each human form of *Himself* with the ability to choose his or her own thoughts, beliefs, and actions.

Another essential dynamic of the game of life is: *cause and effect*. In the East it's called *karma,* a Sanskrit word meaning *"consequence of past action."* It could also mean, *"consequence of one's choice."* It is neither positive nor negative. It's one of the operating procedures of one's own omnipotence.

Because you have *free will,* you can choose to play life from any perspective, but you will experience the consequence of the choices you make.

If you choose to underestimate yours and others' greatness, you will experience a form of "poverty consciousness." You can choose to doubt your omniscience, your friends, your talent, your ability to create, or you can play life from a grateful, abundant perspective—have your burger any way you want it ... have it with cheese, or with *the works*!

You can choose pain, or you can rise up to your inherent courageous magnificence and choose to experience your truly great Self.

As you practice consciously making choices, you will develop more and more faith in your own power to choose.

Your Choices Define Your Destiny

Some ask, "If God exists everywhere and creates everything, how come we have wars, famine, disease, pain and death?" One answer is that God exists in all people, and each has a choice about what he or she wants to believe and what he or she wants to create.

But not everyone knows this is possible. Not everyone wants the same thing. Not everyone longs to know the highest Truth or yearns for peace and harmony. Not everyone is conscious all the time.

Some love drama and the excitement of battle. Others are motivated by power or wealth. Some choose to grow through struggle and physical limitations.

Each of us has his or her own individual challenges through which we choose to grow and evolve, or not.

Thoroughly examine what you think. Notice how your own thoughts can contribute to procrastination, fear, self-doubt and self-criticism, and what interrupts your powerful flow of inner energy.

The sages named this dynamic *duality*: On the one hand, we know we are the God-Self, but on the other, we continue creating mental and emotional distance from God. With negative self-talk we choose to think the same habitual ideas about ourselves. In the same way that no one else can change our minds, no one else is creating those self-doubts.

When we don't trust ourselves and don't give ourselves reasons to follow through with our dreams, we are blocking flows of energy, making it difficult for us to get what we want.

You may ask, "But how can I change these old habits right now?"

You can begin by talking to yourself with kindness, with love and respect: *"Good morning, Self! You've got lots of things to do today, but you can do it! You've gotten this far. You can make it happen! You know that you are, in fact, making your dreams come true as you take each step during the day. Keep at it!"*

Try encouraging yourself, and always remind yourself that you are God in the form of you. Remind yourself of your own power, and practice using your new awareness more and more each day. Re-choose and re-cast every sabotaging thought that comes up in your mind. Mastery comes with practice—with making new choices every day.

Karma, the Law of Cause and Effect

Have you ever had a very angry thought and then immediately walked into a wall or took a wrong turn by mistake?

This is an example of the law of cause and effect. It happens as a consequence of a previous thought—perhaps a negative thought, or maybe simply a distracted one.

Even when we are masters of our minds, we still can't escape the consequences of our thoughts … unless we are very aware and quick!

Being aware of what you are thinking is a first step. If you don't like the thought you just created, let it go, drop it, or transform it immediately. When you understand the dynamic of free will, on the spot you can make a new choice, and avoid manifesting the one you had just "thunk."

As soon as we change the causal thought, we change the effect. As our skills build, we notice we are staying on a *happiness course* more and more often, and we naturally are choosing increasingly peaceful pathways to explore.

Of course, sometimes we've made a choice that feels unchangeable—such as our choice of a mate, choosing to have children, or choosing to remain in a particular career.

But even though we may feel as though we can't change some things about such parts of our lives, we can always choose how we view them, our attitude towards them, and how we behave around them.

We can apply the teaching, "love the one you're with," and see what happens to our inner "happiness meter."

You want to use your life in the most uplifting way, but sometimes you arrive at a particular juncture in life and regret some choices you've made. There is a saying, "No one ever wanted to have his tombstone inscribed with the words, *I wish I'd spent more time at the office*." It's also okay to make new choices.

Don't beat yourself up with regrets. Have compassion for yourself.

Doubting Her Choices

Suzanne felt she had sabotaged herself and her family for over twenty years through the choices she had made. Her kids grew up; her parents, in-laws, and grandparents died. Her beloved niece and brother died. She saw how she had sacrificed relationships with them for habits that were only partially satisfying. She admitted she was a workaholic, often signing up for overtime instead of attending family functions. She loves children, yet never made time to get to know her niece or nephew.

She told me that when she's home she spends her downtime watching, *"way too much television."*

"How do I forgive myself for the choices I've made?" she asked me. *"How do I live with the consequences now? Nearly everyone is dead. Will they forgive me for my choices?"*

I asked her, *"Did you do the best you knew how at the time?"*

"Well, yes," she replied.

"Is there a way for you to make new choices aligned with your new values?" I inquired.

She said, *"I wanted the best for my whole family, even then. I could learn from my past and commit to being more true to myself right now.*

The Courage to Be Happy

Scott was a highly paid salesman working for a large high-tech medical firm. He sold more equipment than anyone and earned a six-figure salary. He loved his job, clients and co-workers, and also enjoyed the freedom to travel. Because he was exceptional at his work, he was offered the position of sales manager. He took the new position after much persuasion by both his parents and co-workers. "Manager" sounded like a more prestigious title to them.

Several weeks into his new position, Scott arrived at my office complaining of severe depression and unhappiness. *"My family will think I'm a loser if I go back to my sales position,"* he admitted.

"How would <u>you</u> feel?" I asked.

"I'd feel true to myself. I loved my job and loved going to work everyday," he replied.

"What have you learned by taking the manager position?" I asked.

He thought for a moment. *"I want to be happy in my work, doing what I'm good at. I paid too much attention to getting approval from my parents and for the wrong reasons. I was afraid to displease them. What I truly want is for them to respect me for being true to myself."*

The sales department was excited to have Scott back. Because he was happier than he'd been in a long time, Scott's family noticed, too, and ended in respecting him for his decision.

Scott's entire family benefited when he found the courage to stand up for himself.

Just Happy

Exercise 9

What are the ingredients of happiness?

Is happiness a result of what you're doing? Is it created by other people? Is it caused by your environment?

Or are your happy feelings generated by the way you look out from your heart?

1. Ask yourself, "Am I in a loving state of mind when I assess a situation? Am I coming from compassion? From gratefulness? From understanding? Or am I coming from suspicion or fear?"
2. Can I remember God is everywhere, in everyone and in every situation? How can I change my inner attitude—the stuff I'm sitting in that's coloring how I see things?
3. What can I do to feel happy in every situation?
4. Every day this week ask yourself, "What is one good thing about this person, this day, this life?"

That one good thing will set happiness in motion.

Loving the Life You Choose

Each of us has an inner emotional guidance system that helps us navigate how close or distant we feel from who and what we love. At times we feel flashes of bliss—signs saying, "This way … this way."

Some have these moments when they're very young and feel directed toward a career that promises more of the same. Whether a football player, designer, musician, cook, artist, engineer, mother, father, builder, doctor, electrician, physicist, computer game designer or programmer—each find joy in the career they have chosen because they listened to that early flash of recognition.

Programmers tell me, "I'm in bliss writing code." Day after day, hour after hour, they sit at their computers writing this complicated esoteric stuff and are totally mesmerized—happy and in bliss. The young man who lives down the street from me feels the same way about playing his guitar, and my sister Betty is *in bliss* digging in her garden.

These fortunate people are able to feel a pure form of God in their work: They've learned to pay attention to their own happiness barometer.

Happiness eludes others. Why? Because they really aren't conscious of the elements within their own self that bring about feelings of joy. People often believe that joy and bliss are caused by external sources. They don't know it's an inside job.

As a beginning saint, when you get an inner "delete" or "burn-out" message from your emotional guidance system, redesign your thoughts and realign them with your God-Self. When you do this, you'll see how your new thought choices create happy consequences. It will become quite apparent that, with your free will, you can initiate, stop, delete or change the direction of any thought at any point on the thought continuum—from the impulse to think the thought, all the way to its manifestation in form.

As soon as we have a thought, we send that creation into the vibration system of the world. If not changed, it will manifest in some form, however subtle.

Many times the thought is exactly what we want to create, but at other times, once we've had the thought and verbalized it, we realize it's not exactly what we had intended. Beyond our awareness was a conflicting thought that created a different result than we had consciously wanted.

When a thought doesn't come to fruition, it can be due to *conflicting intentions* or to an aspect of the original thought that creates a mixed intention.

By recognizing this dynamic, we have the power to stop and change a thought at any time.

How often have you wished for something to come true, but it came with unexpected consequences?

People ask for fame and achieve it, but then experience myriad little irritations—loss of anonymity, pursuing paparazzi, groupies, and more demands on their time and legal issues than they ever imagined.

Responsible wishing will involve the kind of creative thinking that visualizes a full picture of how your desires will materialize, including how your creation will impact yourself, others and the world at large.

As an example, when Suzy created a thought, she included how she wanted it to look, function, and feel: *"Knowing God is everywhere, within everything and everyone, including in me, I choose to have a job that's fascinating, gives my life purpose, is close to home, feels challenging, is not too stressful, and brings me so much abundance that I can financially support projects that are important to me."*

Discipline Leads to Freedom

Saints throughout the ages taught that discipline and mastery are required to build uplifting thinking habits. Without an ability to control and shape thoughts, a person is at the mercy of the prevailing winds. A disciplined mind enables us to live in our God-Self consciousness—in our inseparable relationship with God.

As we develop control over our thinking habits, we develop the ability to focus and refocus our thoughts at will. We gain the skill to plant only those things we really want in the garden of our life.

How many times have you walked away from a movie and said to yourself, *"Why did I sit there and take in all those awful images and feelings for two hours when I could have been playing music with friends or cuddling up with my partner?"*

What about old feelings that seem to pop up out of nowhere? On occasion, my daughter Mia has been known to tell me, "Mom, stop awfulizing!" I usually end up laughing and applauding her creative use of the language, but I'm also startled out of the habit and grateful that she helps me stop thinking that way.

Perhaps it's been years since you felt a certain feeling or sensation. As children we're often bombarded by the feelings and emotions of our family members and their beliefs and ideas.

When this happens, ask yourself, *"What sensation am I feeling now? Where did I first experience this feeling? Who in my family has felt this way? Is it my feeling, or does it really belong to someone else"?*

When you identify where it came from and know it's not yours, the feeling will dissolve.

Remember, your *free will* enables you to stop, let go, and re-intend a thought in order to bring about what you truly want.

You're no longer run by a reactive impulsive mind that's out of control. You are operating your life from your highest and best self, able to discriminate between your own thoughts and the evening news.

Paint with pain and you will get hurt. Paint with criticism and you'll get defensiveness.

Through Beginning Saint you are even discovering the great power you have to quiet your mind and experience a thought free state.

Paint with kindness and you'll get patience. Paint with love and what is reflected back will be love. Watch the colors and sounds you choose. Your painting will reflect the colors and textures you use.

As you develop more skill in choosing your thoughts, you'll experience a huge leap in personal power—greater than you've ever dreamed.

PART II

An Evolution of Consciousness
The Unity of Science and Spirituality

Chapter 6

A Scientific-Spiritual Revolution Is Brewing

In actuality, everyone is looking for *Universal Truth*. Scientists wouldn't be scientists if they weren't looking for the truth of things. Like the saints, scientists have great respect for the unseen.

Philosophers, engineers, artists, naturalists, musicians, doctors, writers, poets, dancers—everyone is searching for Truth, each in his or her own way,

Scientifically based communities across the world are beginning to openly merge theories of science and spirituality, bypassing the seeming boundaries between these disciplines. Many scientists are conducting studies that openly investigate how thought affects the physical form of things.

Such communities are forcing us to expand our concepts of what's real. They're combining the understandings of spirituality, holography and quantum physics, and are challenging old philosophical and scientific beliefs in all areas of our lives.

In the West, a huge renaissance of consciousness began to appear about a hundred and fifty years ago. As travel and communications opened doors to the ancient teachings of the East, Western philosophers and theologians started to explore and introduce them in the West. Simultaneously, scientists in the West were making new discoveries in physics and medicine that resonated with these spiritual teachings.

In the late 1800s, the East Indian saint, Sri Yukteshwar, in his book *The Holy Science*, wrote, *"The Earth has already moved into a period of awakening, a Yuga of light, which will last for two thousand years. It is a time when human beings have developed the capacity to understand the five sorts of electricity."*

He said, *"Now, in this 194th year of Dwapara Yuga, the dark age of Kali having long since passed, the world is reaching out for spiritual knowledge, and men require loving help one from the other."*

He continued, *"There is an essential unity in all religions. There is no real discrepancy, much less any real conflict between the teachings of the East and West. We have entered an age of rapid development in all areas of man's knowledge, where man's intellect can finally begin to grasp the highest understanding."*

Americans have experienced many revolutions since the 1960s: the Civil Rights Movement, the Feminist Movement, the Sexual Revolution, the Ecology Movement, the Bio-Pharmaceutical Revolution, and the Information Revolution. These revolutions have led to many great personal and cultural freedoms and to a vast expansion of the reach of humankind.

I became aware of both the positive and negative consequences of these revolutions in the lives of an amazing assortment of ethnic, cultural, social and family groups where I lived.

Comprising extraordinarily bright young people with exceptional educations, exciting careers, and extremely abundant incomes, these groups had more personal power than any middle-class generation in the world at the time. They could afford the best food, health care, housing and technology, and were politically and economically free to pursue their dreams. They enjoyed freedoms that others only dream of.

However, in their mad race to acquire degrees and careers, houses and children, these people let the teachings of their childhood spiritual traditions recede. Even though engaged in the most abstract forms of scientific thought, few consciously investigated their own internal spiritual center, unless confronted with the death of a friend or close family member, or when a life event forced them to ask, "What does it all mean?"

Today, an essential and dynamic revolution is taking place, "The Exploration of the Power of the Mind." Those previous revolutions I mentioned that had provided for so much abundance and social freedom in the United States had not answered the most important questions in life: "Who am I? Where am I going? What is the purpose of my own individual existence? Why do I do the same things year in and year out? How do I control my negative thoughts? There must be an underlying purpose for my life beyond survival."

In *The Cultural Creatives, How 50 Million People Are Changing the World,* Paul Ray and Sherry Anderson ask just such questions and express a great optimism about the future. They delineate the positive steps being taken by over fifty million people living around the world who are individually and collectively taking responsibility for making their lifestyles congruent with what they value.

Ray and Anderson define "Cultural Creatives" as individuals who work in many different fields, all with the goal of helping both Mother Earth and her inhabitants live healthier, happier, more sustainable lifestyles.

The authors suggest that the integral culture of the future will include increasingly idealistic social institutions, where values and beliefs will come from a "synthesis of expanded consciousness." They tell us, "Concrete changes in the world will follow automatically from changes in our attitudes and beliefs about who we are."

The worldwide shift in consciousness that Yukteshwar predicted has begun. There is already a big difference between the world of yesteryear and the world of the future—one where millions of human beings actually experience themselves consciously as God in thought and action.

Seekers ask, "Who really knows the ultimate Truth? Should I trust my parents, my friends—the teachers I've had so far in my life? Have they offered me understanding that feels deeply true to me? Where do I look for answers?"

A self-realized saint points you to your own *inner Guru*, your inner Self. However, until you have complete trust in your own knowing, inner discipline and realizations, the most valuable thing you can do is to find such a self-realized saint—someone who has attained the highest state himself or herself.

The search is essential. Asking people you respect—teachers and friends whose life and thinking you admire—is key.

Ask them how they developed their understanding. Try on teachings yourself. Feel how such teachings resonate with your own inner understandings. On your spiritual path, pay attention to your own inner intuition and feelings.

While searching for your personal Guru, do what you can to expand your own consciousness. As a beginning saint you are learning to do this. Remind yourself of your own true identity, realizing your own individual purpose, and committing to maintaining the highest awareness of yourself and others.

The Best Preventive Medicine

Realizing You Are Always Making a Choice

Your power to choose is the most powerful medicine. Healthy choices are key to emotional and physical well-being. Choice is always superior to blame. With choice you can create a world of joy and harmony—or agitation and disharmony. It's all up to you.

Doctors of alternative medicine tell me that those who come for treatment for physical and mental health have often suffered a lifetime of intense emotion, including stored anger and fear. These practitioners work to bring consciousness to their clients regarding the habitual emotional feedback loops that contribute to disease.

Sometimes a client learns the origin of the illness and how to emotionally release the stuck energy causing it. Other times the client learns how to rebalance his or her own *emotional guidance system*. Sometimes, on the other hand, because the human body was designed to heal itself, healing happens even without understanding.

With conscious practice, however, a person can learn to automatically correct chronic states and take responsibility for his or her own health.

Do Opinions and Judgments Get in Our Way?

One day I was listening to an author being interviewed on public radio. I remember him saying, "I don't think good literature can be written in Florida, California or Hawaii.

Writers who live in cold snowy climates know what tragedy, pain and harsh winters are all about. How can you be a good writer if you only know sunshine?"

Do you agree with that idea?

Notice how *opinion* is a form of decision or choice. It is a choice to perceive something in a certain way. Opinions are forms of beliefs that expand or contract our perspective.

We can agree with that author's opinion, but we can also choose to let go of that opinion and think a new thought—one that allows great writers to live anywhere.

One of our most significant choices, once we know we are a perfect *ray* of God, is whether or not to operate our lives from God's widest, freest perspective.

Are you choosing in every moment to live in the light?

The most powerful thing to know about *free will* is that, once you intend something to happen, it will in fact manifest unless you interrupt or change its direction.

A corollary in science is Newton's First Law: "An object in motion will remain in motion unless acted upon by an equal and opposite force."

That's why it's so important to be aware of exactly what you *are* intending, including all the surrounding subtle thoughts that sometimes sabotage your original intention. Be aware how even subtle thoughts and tiny attitude impulses can affect your destiny, and how important it is to consciously shape them.

Notice that when you think flowing, peaceful thoughts you feel close to your God-Self, and when you think angry or fearful thoughts you feel more distant.

How the Mind Affects the Body

Mastering our minds brings physical as well as emotional health. When we root out unwanted thoughts, we are mastering the field of preventive medicine, at least within ourselves.

When you notice an uncomfortable feeling, learn to quickly identify the causal thought and change or drop it. Notice whether the idea is coming from your *small self* or from your *God-Self.*

Identifying the source of the thought will enable you to quickly eject any mistaken belief and clarify what you really want.

Choosing only those thoughts that come from the *God-Self* is the path to the magnificent, healthy and masterful being you really are.

At some point in the past you may have forfeited your power in a relationship by doubting yourself or minimizing your own natural knowing. Discounting yourself frequently manifests in a blocked flow. Sometimes this appears as muscle tension, sometimes as a cold, sometimes as colitis, sometimes as a headache, etc.

When you remember you are the God-Self, divinely expressing in the world, you automatically release limiting thoughts of yourself. Standing up for yourself, in a kind but firm way, frees your body to release tension and increase strength. You are learning that your health is dependent on what you feed your mind.

Practicing remembering your God-Self increases your ability to manage your spiritual immune system in order to stay healthy, and demonstrates that your health truly is in large part dependent on what you feed your mind.

We see the emotional consequences of our thoughts return to us in a feedback loop, from our minds to our bodies to our environments and back. When we feel happy, enthusiastic, or peaceful, our bodies feel energetic and our blood is circulating oxygen, reaching all the cells. We get immediate feedback from our own bodies, which helps us stay healthy.

Your body is your great friend. If you listen to it, it helps you maintain overall health. It lets you know when it has had enough of anything. It tells you when things are out of order in your everyday life. If your relationships are troubled, if your work life is out of order—if you feel powerless in any way—your body tells you.

You have the ability to take action in both your own inner world of mind and body and in your external world. As you pay attention to what your body is telling you, you'll let go of old programs and make new choices. You'll experience feeling the difference between helplessness and power.

Thoughts Become Things?

Your mind allows you to be the designer of your life, but unless you realize its worth, it's like driving a BMW convertible in Los Angeles traffic at 5:00 p.m. — in spite of having a great vehicle, you have no power to go anywhere.

In an effort to pack a hundred things into his day, a friend of mine always found himself canceling dinner plans with friends or being embarrassingly late. Unknowingly his choices ended up making him feel out of control and alienating his friends.

We can feel out of control when we allow old habits, or everyone and everything else, to choose for us.

With out of control thoughts, habits, or judgments our hearts automatically start beating faster, our blood pressure rises, and our bodies switch into survival mode.

When we think peaceful thoughts, on the other hand, our bodies vibrate more sweetly, our heart rate slows down, and we feel happy and peaceful inside.

The Computer and the Mind

Then there are those darn "pop ups." What to do about them? On the computer we can simply press the "Delete" button.

In life, however, when unexpected events "pop up," knocking us off our center, we need a whole toolbox of wrenches, pliers, ropes and glue "to put Humpty Dumpty (in this case, our minds) back together again."

This is one of the great challenges of all spiritual seekers—in fact, of all human beings.

Quantum physicists are just beginning to delve into the directive power of humankind's thoughts—something the East has known about all along. Eastern masters have demonstrated that knowing how the mind works is the best basis for building a health-maintenance system.

When we instantaneously know our thoughts are out of kilter and rebalance ourselves, we also manage and buoy our physical immune systems. When we create joyous, expansive thoughts, we also experience great energy in our bodies. We *are* in charge.

Beginning saints learn to recognize when their thoughts originate from a faulty belief or limited idea of themselves or another. They quickly weed out any mistaken beliefs, programming, and misunderstandings about who they are, and clarify what it is they want to retain.

The next great achievement of science will be the understanding of the mental and spiritual abilities latent in man. When we believe something can't possibly happen, we are essentially saying 'no' to its manifestation. On the other hand, when we believe in the possibility of something, we give it permission to happen in our lives.

—Charles Fillmore

In his book, *Atom Smashing Power of Mind,* Charles Fillmore taught, "Thoughts do become things. Every creative thing began with a thought."

This is how it works: Every thought you think creates a vibration and a consequence. When you think a thought, express a desire, or breathe a prayer, the universe produces what you tell it.

However, when you don't want what you asked for, it's essential that you know you can stop an order altogether—or change it—to get what you truly want. Even unconscious underlying beliefs and assumptions can materialize when we least expect them.

A friend of mine who's working on correcting her thoughts often shouts "Delete! Delete!" whenever her thoughts veer off into an undesirable direction.

When an idea takes form in the mind, it first arises as an impulse or inspiration. Then the thought takes form in words or images, the words or images have meanings, and these create feelings that become our experience.

It's like ordering a pizza: Visualize what you want, including all the toppings. Imagine how it will taste. Imagine how it will feel in your tummy.

Then place the order by describing it to the waiter, and trust that it's on its way.

We've had lots of practice placing orders in restaurants and phoning in orders for "take out," but sometimes we do not realize that the same principle works with our own omnipotent God-Self: The moment we think a thought, our thought-creation is already in process.

Know that your all-powerful God-Self is manifesting your thought-creation simultaneously as you think it. Know that God always delivers your request, along with the best outcome for everyone involved.

To our God-Self, there are no impossible situations or answers.

We can allow ourselves to receive the gifts of the thought even before we see them in three-dimensional form. We can be grateful for this new knowledge—what is truly a profound shift in consciousness. The more we trust this process, the more extraordinary our results.

Diana Learns to Place Orders

In a quiet moment at home, Diana *"placed an order"* for her business to expand. She thought, "Knowing that God is fully present within me and in everyone related to my business, and knowing that nothing can limit my God-Self from producing what I want, I see my business flourishing, providing me with abundant customers, fun, and friendship."

Then she went about making business contacts, phone calls and making room for that abundance to show up, trusting that nothing could get in her way but her own thoughts. Month after month, new business opened up to her, and by tax time she realized she had brought in over $350,000 in net sales.

Of course, placing an order can be about any subject at all. We may want to ask for friendship, for the ability to control a habit, or to understand an interpersonal dynamic. We might ask the universe for something as mundane as "just a little time," or for a new pair of shoes.

The trick is getting clear about what we are asking for, and trusting with conviction that our innate power to "ask and you shall receive" is valid, and not going into doubt about the teaching. "It's important to remind yourself that "in the universe everything already exists. All I need to do is claim it as my own."

Manifesting

Exercise 10

1. Sit quietly by yourself, close your eyes and take a few slow breaths in and out through your nose.
2. Consider something you want to have, do or be.
3. Imagine how you want it to look, feel, and function.
4. Envision how you would like it to show up in your life.
5. Imagine it happening—right now, with full sounds, smells and sensations.
6. Add, "Thank you God-Self for manifesting this or something even greater," Now, expect that it's on its way.

But what If I don't have a focused mind and very strong intention. … What if doubtful thoughts arise too? What do I do with those?

When that occurs, notice what you are thinking. Notice the feeling of the thought in your body. Gently ask yourself, "Is that a thought I want to think?"

If the answer is "no," allow yourself to let go of the old thought and replace it with one you would like to think instead. You could envision the old thought floating off on the next cloud in the sky. You might imagine dropping the old thought in a wastebasket or creatively bursting it like a bubble so that it contains no more doubting energy. Now, allow yourself to think the new thought, and release it to your highest God-Self to create instead.

Psychoneuroimmunology

Psychoneuroimmunology is the interaction between psychological processes and the nervous and immune systems of the body, and is one of the reasons that the mind can keep the body's immune system healthy. This interaction is a function of perfect health, works automatically, and is directly related to the content of our thoughts.

As you observe this dynamic, you'll discover ways you've actually sabotaged your power in the past by doubting yourself or minimizing the truth of your own natural knowing, or by failing to persist with your dreams.

The saints teach that a person's mind functions on a spectrum of consciousness from dark to light.

The first level or state of mind consists of a deep, dark, heaviness—a sluggish state of awareness and being in the world.

The next state is full of action and energy. It's considered the normal state of a human being who is unaware of his or her divinity.

The final state is very pure—it is the saint's awareness—free, light, loving. It is a happy, blissful state of light, intelligence and wisdom.

The state of one's physical health corresponds with the state of one's consciousness. When your mind and life are centered in pure love and awareness, your immune system physically reflects this centeredness.

It only makes sense!

Practice a Healthy Mind, a Healthy Body

Stop It, Drop It, Change It

I used to wonder, "Why did I create that thought?" Our thoughts are frequently both unconscious, out of our awareness, and habitual. When we identify a destructive thought and either let it go or replace it with a new thought, we gain power over it. We can stop it, drop it, or change it.

The understanding of quantum physics shows us how the power of the placebo effect can transform our health. The placebo effect shows us that our beliefs are stronger than any apparent condition we've given power to.

My husband, Bruce, is a physician who was trained as a medical doctor, but now has a private alternative-healing practice. He utilizes a healing method that supports the individual's own healing power to do the work. With this approach, even when problems have been chronic, the shift often occurs rapidly within a single visit.

He tells his clients, *"Only the soul can heal so quickly."* Bruce refrains from offering a diagnosis. He says, "A medical diagnosis often leads to a mental construct that solidifies into a belief. When a diagnosis is shared with those who know the client, friends and family then reinforce the belief and the problem can feel energetically frozen. "I see symptoms as 'an uneasiness.' The uneasiness in the body or emotions is a message to look for the path of ease, back into the wholeness and wellness that already exists within.

"Our body, our faithful servant, was given the job to carry that which we cannot or will not deal with at a given time. Like a faithful servant on a long safari, the body is carrying that burden, waiting for us to come back to release it, rest and restore it. Sometimes, however, we have become unaware that we left this burden on the body."

Bruce sees his job as supporting the client's release of outward symptoms while helping the client to be true to his or her true divine nature.

He says, *"As an individual consciously takes responsibility for this inner work, the unconscious need for the physical symptom dissolves. At the heart of this work is the release of blocked energy and symptoms, which were caused by mistaken core beliefs—those out of alignment with the client's divine nature. With resolution, the symptoms and energy are freed and can be used for productivity, creativity, and quality of life."*

He continues, "When emotions get blocked, suppressed or forced, they also constrict flows of communication between people, and correspondingly shut down feelings in the body. And, whether restricted flows or torrents, emotions can cause damage both in relationships and in the body. Transforming a stuck thought breaks the cycle between the thought and its manifestation in a physical form. Even very subtle thoughts influence the body."

Adopting the perspective of a *beginning saint,* you create a brand-new flow, thereby coming into the higher inner awareness of your God-Self. This sets in motion the manifestation of a new positive condition or situation in life. The body's balance is re-established, and with it, a new, energetic, healthy equilibrium.

Reversing Health Conditions

Exercise 11

To release negative ideas, thoughts, and beliefs contributing to a health condition, ask yourself these questions:

1. Are there any unwanted physical or emotional situations in my life now? (If none, celebrate! Only do this exercise at a time a symptom shows up.)
2. Identify a symptom. What do I feel?
3. When did I start to experience this condition?
4. What are the characteristics of this condition, i.e. pain in my joints, stomach hurts, weakness, etc.?
5. What thoughts, beliefs (about what mental or physical conditions might have caused it), situations, or judgments in my life could be contributing to the emotional and/or physical condition I am, or have been, experiencing?
6. Did I have an emotional upset with someone in my life 24-48 hours prior to the condition showing up?
7. If so, what was the upset about? With whom was I upset? What decisions or ideas did I make that limited me? What communication did I suppress with that person? What flow got stuck?
8. What did I keep myself from communicating to that person? What are all the things I wanted to say or do instead? (Admit all of it, particularly to yourself.)

9. Notice how you feel now.
10. If you find yourself laughing, congratulate yourself—laughing is one form of release.

Thought Affects One's Energy Field

An article in *China Healthways* Newsletter, Spring 2000, states: "Strong emotions cause chronic illness, advance aging and impede healing by warping the human energy field. If our emotional being (Qi) is clear, it manifests our ideals perfectly in the physical. By becoming aware of, and then dissolving and releasing that which clouds the emotional body, we can open the door to symptomatic relief and accelerated recovery. When we can clear our Qi, our emotional body, of counter-productive and life-distorting emotional issues, healing is accelerated and chronic pain is often relieved. Life becomes more purposeful, joyful, and fulfilling."

Your ability to prevent illness is enhanced when you power yourself with the most loving, accurate thoughts of yourself and others. The bottom line of prevention is reclaiming your view of yourself as whole, healthy and masterful.

In Chapter 10 you will learn how to use the "Beginning Saint Bridge," an even more immediate process of clearing away upsetting thoughts and beliefs.

Remember, you are already the God-Self, divinely expressing in the world as the person you are.

The Psychological Prevention and Treatment of the Common Cold

Studies of quantum physics, string theory and the theory of holographic unity suggest your thoughts affect both the state of your physical health and how successful you are in life. They've shown how thoughts not only affect one's individual physical body, but the culture at large. They imply that what you think and feel impacts others at a subatomic level, whether you have ever met them or not.

Have you heard of "*The Hundredth Monkey*?" The story describes an evolutionary process that occurs when one single animal learns a task and that learning is transmitted, at an unconscious level, to the entire species. It points to how interconnected we are to each other and to the planet as a whole.

Science and spirituality are coming together—verifying the teachings of the sages and spiritual masters in light of a new cosmology, bringing all teachings together, and making sense of them. Each teaches that you are made of the same energy that spins the planets, opens the flowers, makes your heart beat and your breath flow.

Right now, you are developing the ability to change your mind at will and the skills necessary to maintain a healthy life. When you are aware of what's happening both inside of you and outside of you, you've taken another step to having true power in your life.

In 1988 I wrote my doctoral dissertation to verify an experience I had had with a friend a decade earlier. What had happened was so profound for me, I remember thinking, "This is like Jesus walking on water."

On a rainy fall evening I had been suffering from a terrible cold. I could barely talk. My throat hurt fiercely, and my nose was runny, but I showed up for dinner anyway. My friend Isabelle asked me, "Do you want to get rid of your cold?"

I thought it an odd question, but immediately answered, "Yes."

"Good," she replied. "Have you had an upset with anyone during the past 24-48 hours?"

At first I replied, "No," but then immediately recalled a communication break with a friend the day before where I found out she had been lying to me. I failed to tell her openly and directly my real thoughts and feelings about how betrayed I felt.

Isabelle proceeded to ask me a series of five questions, all designed for me to finally express the thoughts and feelings I had withheld from my friend. Right in the middle of the question-asking process, I found myself laughing hilariously and my sore throat absolutely gone. My runny nose was gone, too. I felt totally well.

I felt I had discovered a new revolutionary healing mechanism. I attributed *the cure* to the moment I felt completely free to express all my thoughts and feelings openly to her.

Several years later I grabbed the opportunity to investigate this *"cold process"* for my doctoral dissertation research. I entitled it, *The Psychological Prevention and Treatment of the Common Cold*. I wanted to understand the underlying dynamic Isabelle had performed on me so many years earlier. My hypothesis was, "Common cold symptoms develop as a result of withheld stuck communications and dissolve through free-flowing, open communication." It's that simple.

How our thoughts affect our physical body, the negative effects of stress, and how to transform the whole chain of reactions pointed me to the literature on psychoneuroimmunology. I was excited by the book *Getting Well Again* by O. Carl Simonton and Stephanie Matthews-Simonton, where they suggested that cancer, as well as other illnesses, has evolved in response to perceived life stressors seen as uncontrollable.

They wrote, "All of us create the meaning of events in our lives. The individual who assumes the victim stance participates by assigning meanings to life events that prove there is no hope. Each of us chooses—although not always at a conscious level—how we are going to react. The intensity of the stress is determined by the meaning we assign to it and the rules we have established for how we will cope with stress."

I explored many other healing traditions that demonstrated how negative thoughts, beliefs, and mental attitudes have a deleterious effect on the human body.

However, like those of many fledgling researchers, the statistical results of my research were only "in the direction" of proving my hypothesis. But I found that when a person's sense of control of his life is restored, his immune system is also immediately restored.

Also, a surprising variable showed up. Out of the 400 subjects I studied, several reported they simply didn't have time to get a cold. They had made a very clear choice, *I will not get a cold no matter what,* and they didn't.

When I shared this data with a lawyer friend of mine, she confirmed that the same statistics show up among her lawyer cohorts. She said that the attorneys she knew told her they don't have time to get ill. *"Many of them get sick on vacation instead."*

My own research over the years has revealed that the body's ability to heal itself is related to a person's conviction or lack of conviction that he is in control of his life. If he feels free to communicate, he will be a physically and mentally healthier person. He will know he has the freedom to "speak up" or take charge if he chooses.

At a spiritual level, I believe that if a person has the stable conviction that she is the God-Self, with all of the qualities and powers of God, she will be more confident that she knows what to do and how to do it. She will feel more assertive and empowered in life.

In the 1970s, stress researcher Martin Seligman demonstrated how this dynamic works. He confirmed the concept of *learned helplessness* in an experiment where he divided two groups of dogs. He gave one the ability to control the amount and time in which he ate. The other group had no control over their food supply.

He found the animals that remained healthy were ones who were given control over their feeding schedules. When dogs perceived they had no control over their feeding schedule, they just gave up and died.

Over the years, since I learned the dynamics of the *cold process* and have practiced the knowing of a beginning saint, I've noticed my own immune system getting stronger. I very rarely experience colds or get sick.

When it does happen, I try to identify the causal belief, express the withheld communication, and turn it around. Usually my immune system is restored within minutes.

Ultimately, healing doesn't have to do with changing conditions in the world. Healing happens when your thoughts are triumphantly and purposefully tuned to your true God-identity, which is totally healthy, whole, and free from limitations.

Within the healing process you release ideas of limitation and feelings of lack of control. You move your consciousness to the highest truth, and the condition, the physical illness, the lack of money, job, or relationship—shifts to a higher state.

The subjects in my study who did not get colds had taken charge of their lives. They used a cognitive behavioral technique called "thought stopping." Through their conviction they had the power to direct their thoughts. Their bodies responded accordingly.

Whether we are aware of it or not, the universe always gives us what we are choosing.

It's good to reflect on what choices you are making and recognize any conflicting intentions.

How often do you say, "I'm sick and tired of work," and then proceed to get the flu, which forces you to bed?

How many times do you say, "I really want to lose ten pounds," and then you go ahead and have cheesecake for dessert?

What if you said to yourself, "I'm losing ten pounds and I'm having cheesecake for dessert?"

As you gain command of your mind, you'll notice some of your thoughts affecting your physical body. The feeling may show up as a headache, poor posture, a pain in your neck, diarrhea or anxiety.

Notice how what you think affects your physical health and lifestyle in general. What is the relationship between your thoughts and your feelings?

When you confront an unwanted thought and choose an alternative such as, "I let go of all previous thoughts of limitation and choose to see infinite options ahead for me," at that very moment you are changing the course of your health and your life.

There is no rush—everything happens in its own perfect time. The universe is always in perfect order, but sometimes we can't see it.

You will notice that the more you consciously choose what you think, the more control you will have of both your emotional and physical world.

Perhaps you are already seeing the benefits of taking charge. You're learning you can uproot those old mental pictures and replace them with relaxed thoughts, ease, gentleness and peacefulness.

How Our Thoughts Affect Our Life And Jazz Pizzazz

Jerry was very self-conscious about his piano playing. He was fluid and happy when he played for himself but, for most of his life, when asked to perform for others he would scrunch up his shoulders, tighten his fists, stomach and legs, and become almost paralyzed with fear.

One day I happened to secretly catch him playing by himself. He was relaxed, feeling happy, flowing, with a provocative style all his own. I could not believe the difference in his music.

One day I asked him to pretend he was playing only for himself. Interestingly, the more he pretended, the more he enjoyed playing. The more he pretended, the more expressive he became, and the more playful and joyful he felt. I noticed that every once in a while when his shoulders were up to his ears, he would purposely relax them himself and take a long breath before each song he played.

The last I heard, Jerry was performing with two different bands at a local jazz club and having the time of his life.

Help Them Shift Their Attention

Parents often come to me for help with their kindergarteners who are afraid to go to school. Their child is usually feeling either shy or anxious.

I ask them to help their child choose a gift he could give each classmate the next day. If the gift is something to eat, I make sure the parent gets the permission of the teacher and to make sure it's safe for all the children in the classroom. I ask parents to help create the gift with their child. It might require them to purchase enough cookies, or to find enough rocks or stickers for everyone.

The next day when the child goes to school, instead of feeling fear, his anxious thoughts are replaced and focused instead on giving. The child has a special time during the school day to share his presents with his classmates.

It always works. Several things happen. The child's self esteem is increased, because she has become the giver and is in charge. She has direct interaction with each classmate. In the process of giving, she develops courage and self esteem. From the first day, school becomes a positive place where she feels good about herself.

Jesus' teaching, *"As you believe, so it shall be done unto you,"* tells us how our minds work. We attract whatever we believe is true. If we believe we can make something happen, the equivalent of that thought will manifest. If we believe it is difficult to make something happen, the same will be true.

The reason to understand this dynamic is that we are always manifesting what we think. It is simply another validation of how important it is for us to recognize what perceptions and beliefs are running us.

We need to know not only how to construct and delete a thought, but how to maintain positive constructive thoughts as well. We first focus our attention, and then create a clear thought along with the feelings that we want to accompany the thought.

For example, a young woman named Stephanie wanted to present ideas for a new product to her co-workers. She visualized herself preparing the talk and her audience liking and accepting the product, but one element was missing. She had omitted how she wanted to physically and emotionally *feel* during the presentation.

When she recognized she had not considered that element, she re-envisioned herself feeling self-confident, energetic, playful, fluid and capable.

The doctrine of *mental equivalents, "As you believe, so shall it be done unto you,"* invites each of us to dream bigger and to design our life as magnificently as we can.

Anxiety and Panic Attacks Are Great Teachers—

What Are They and How Do I Get Rid of Them?

Dr. Herbert Benson, the father of "stress research" in the West, was able to describe the way the mind triggers the body's *fight-or-flight mechanism*, which in turn creates specific cellular responses in the body. He taught students how to use their own breath to regulate their body, and called it *the relaxation response*. He showed students how to control their heartbeats, cardiovascular systems, and musculature by focusing on their breathing and progressively relaxing their bodies as their breath moved gently and slowly in and out.

Saints and sages from both Buddhist and Hindu meditation traditions have taught these same relaxation processes for thousands of years. Along with the amazing ability to control the body's built-in *fight-or-flight response* is the revelation that habitual thought patterns actually create corresponding agitating or calming reactions in our bodies.

This process could be called, *sensing the Divine Presence in every thought and act.* Your body is a great physical meter for your thoughts. It registers how comfortable you feel with what is going on around you and how you interpret what you are experiencing. Your intuition is your subtle meter for receiving information you might not know using thought alone. You can learn to read your inner meters, like compasses, helping you to move in the healthiest and happiest direction.

Notice yourself what happens when someone calls you a hurtful name. How does your body respond? Does it become tight or tense? Do you push the feeling down, inhibit or rationalize it? Do you withdraw and shut down? Or do you stand up for yourself or fight back?

Are you able to gently let go of reacting at all, or are you on a defensive, reactive high alert? Ideally you are aware of the God Presence in the other, and forgive him for his limited perception of you.

Rebalancing your own mind, your own God-Self, and returning yourself to the truth of who you are, is the best correction you can make. Getting your mind to go where you want it to go requires practice, practice, and more practice.

Sometimes you may feel your mind is running the whole show. People with panic attacks and all kinds of anxiety disorders feel this way. Their imaginations become fantastically prolific. They creatively scare themselves over almost anything.

I often teasingly tell my clients that I'm going to send them to Hollywood to write horror movies because they are so good at creating the most terrible visions in their own minds. Their fearful thoughts ignite physical reactions in their bodies that frighten them.

When that occurs, they're off to see the doctor to find out if they're dying of some rare disease, having a heart attack, or going crazy. With their catastrophic thinking they've decided something is really wrong with their heart, their throat, their stomach, and they want to know why they can't breathe. They believe they are going to die any minute.

Telling a person with panic attacks that it's all in his head is of no value. When a person is in the midst of anxiety or a panic attack, he is experiencing real physiological reactions. He truly may feel dizzy or experience his heart pumping a million miles an hour.

When the body is screaming for attention via unusual emotional and physical sensations, it's difficult to feel in control in one's life. It's like being on a horse that is galloping towards a cliff. People experiencing panic attacks feel powerless to still their minds and breathe. Yet these are the very things they need to do in order to regain control in the moment of panic.

Learning how to control anxiety and panic is one of the most empowering abilities one can have, because when you master anxiety and panic, you have the absolute assurance that you hold the reins of your own mind.

Experiencing panic attacks is actually a tremendous gift. When you've mastered them, you're on your way to mastering your mind. When you learn to stop, change or redirect a thought, you learn that you are absolutely in charge of not only your body, but your life.

Stop Scaring Yourself

Exercise 12

Whether or not you are experiencing panic attacks yourself, you may want to know what you can do to let go of them or assist a friend or family member with them. Here is a process you can use to predictably stop scaring yourself and take charge of your own mind and body.

1. Find a quiet, comfortable place to sit.
2. Stop, shake out your hands, roll your shoulders back, releasing the tension in your hands, neck and back, and breathe … gently in and gently out.
3. Notice the physical sensations you are feeling. They may be very uncomfortable. Just notice them and know that they are not going to kill you or injure you in any way. (Cardiologists actually ask their patients to gradually increase their heart rate as a way of helping the heart become stronger.)
4. Take a deep breath in and hold it at the top of the breath to the count of four: ONE and TWO and THREE and FOUR, and
5. Then exhale very slowly as though you are exhaling all the way down to your toes. Do not hold your breath after an exhalation.
6. Take in a second breath the same way, holding it at the top of the breath to the count of four, and exhale slowly and long, repeating the process of inhaling, holding to the count of four and exhaling long and slowly. Do the breathing eight more times. If you are a little lightheaded, you may be taking in either too much oxygen or not exhaling long

enough. Try to balance the intake of breath with the exhalation. The primary reason for all of the "funny" sensations is the imbalance of the breath. When your incoming and outgoing breaths are balanced, all of the other symptoms will go away.

7. Continue this process until your breath calms down, your heart slows to its natural rhythm, and you are feeling more comfortable inside.

The whole dynamic of panic attacks is actually an indication that your adrenal system is working perfectly. It has just gotten out of your awareness, and by scaring yourself you have set up a habit that keeps the physical symptoms going until you actively take charge by slowing down and balancing your own breath.

With practice, the entire condition will dissolve. When you have the experience and trust that you can stop the panic attacks, they will automatically decrease in number until they go away altogether.

Remind yourself of your indwelling God-Self working perfectly within you at all times.

New Games and Purposes

Once I realized it truly is possible for the average person to understand and develop the skill to create his or her dreams, I was struck by how many of us, it seems, haven't really stretched our imagining capacity very much. We tend to create from the repertoire of the past instead of taking a leap to a totally new dimension. I pondered how great it would be to create a workshop for people to learn how to expand their ability to create.

No sooner had I thought it than I opened my mailbox to find a brochure describing just such a course in Seattle. Created and taught by Dr. Richard Bartlett, the course, called "Matrix Energetics," shows students how to *blow our minds* past preconceived ideas of what it's possible to create.

I signed up.

During one of Dr. Bartlett's classes I learned to simply take a pain in one part of my body and place it outside of my body.

The very fact that this could happen shattered my belief system. The pain left and has never returned. It took me only ten seconds to do it.

Other such trainings are being developed as I write. Mark Dunn, ND, offers a course titled, "Conscious Systems, Tools for Spiritual Living," a series of life-skills trainings for those who want to expand their innate powers.

Meeting Buckminster Fuller

No subject is taboo for seekers of Truth, because they know that God exists in all aspects of life, and that what we call "death" is simply a transition from one experience to another. We experience a similar transition every morning when we wake up from a dream state to a waking state.

Back in the 1980s, I was invited to a lecture given by the brilliant scientist and architect Buckminster Fuller, then in his nineties, at the old Jack Tar Hotel in San Francisco. "Bucky," as he was affectionately called, shared the following insights.

"My dear students, I do not think that I am going to live a whole lot longer and I want to share some ideas with you before I go. I especially want you to understand that this life we are experiencing is not the only reality, not the only plane of existence. You know how dogs can hear sounds that we humans cannot hear. Well, the same is true about energy. These bodies are like radio transistors. You and I can communicate with each other because we have the same kind of transister and antennas. But that doesn't mean that there are not other forms of life on other planes of existence, perhaps moving simultaneously around us right now. Our bodies have been designed with a certain level of sensitivity that we are not aware of. But at this very moment there are probably many radio waves at different frequencies, moving in and through us as well.

I believe that I will continue to live after this life on a plane of existence that we cannot see at this time."

Bucky was an explorer of both inner and outer worlds. His insights corresponded to the teachings of many saints who point to our eternal nature and the ongoing infinite expressions of life.

Mind Is the Root
of Bondage and Liberation,
of Good and Evil,
of Sin and Holiness.

—Bhagawan Nityananda
Nitya Sutra 71

Chapter 7

Make Your Mind Your Friend

Horseback Riding: A Great Teacher of the Mind

Have you ever been horseback riding? Do you remember the first time you ever got on a horse? If you do, you'll remember that the horse probably didn't want to go where you wanted to go.

Neither did my horse. He didn't want to go anywhere. He just wanted to nibble grass on the side of the path. I sighed, "Now what?"

An amused cowboy saw me and yelled, "Just kick him and say, 'Giddy-up!'"

I was horrified. Kick him? No one in my life ever told me to kick anything! I had to take charge of the situation but had no idea how to do so. The reins were in my hands, but I felt powerless.

That's how our minds feel until we know how to take the reins and speak powerfully to our minds. Eventually we gather the courage to say, "Giddy-up, mind, I want to think this thought, not that one."

From a beginning saint's perspective, we want to be able to move our awareness from our limited "small self" to our higher God-Self perspective. Doing that requires having the ability to think, stop, and change our thoughts.

Until we develop the skill of shifting our thoughts and our consciousness, we will be tossed around in the saddle or stopped altogether on our path through life. What we each want is to be in charge of our minds and to feel free to create our own choices, instead of being like puppets on a string, always at the mercy of our distracted minds.

How Your Thoughts Work

When you think peaceful or happy thoughts, your whole body vibrates more sweetly. Your heart rate slows down and you feel happy and content inside.

When you're having anxious, scary, or upsetting thoughts, your heart beats faster, your blood pressure rises, and your body moves into survival mode.

The saints tell us that the vibrations and meanings contained within words form tendencies and emotional attitudes. Developmental biologists call these energy states *morphogenetic* or *morphic fields.* These energy fields act as blueprints for our DNA, which in turn tells our bodies what to make. Similar fields of energy form our beliefs, judgments, and emotions, and resonate with and show up in our physical bodies.

The manifestations of this energy correspond to the levels of peacefulness or agitation of our thoughts. If we are having peaceful thoughts, we feel calm. If we are having agitated thoughts, our bodies tense up and we can manifest all degrees of psychological symptoms such as anxiety, fear, or depression.

Each of us has developed certain judgments of ourselves and then operated in life from those assumptions and decisions. What we think, we become. Life automatically supports our powerful ideas about ourselves by concretizing them in the body and in our circumstances.

If we say to ourselves, "I'm a failure," the world abundantly mirrors this statement. The thought stated this way—as a generalization about ourselves—takes form in several areas of our lives, not just one.

If instead we transform the thought by saying something like, *"You are Divine and embody all of God's wonderful characteristics,"* we experience a whole different attitudinal field.

We are learning to live from our God-Self more every day. Feel the difference in the above two opposing attitudes as you read them. They each are powerful, but the energy field of the first thought produces very different results in the mind and body from that of the second thought.

As the Bible says, *"In the beginning was the Word, and the Word was with God, and the Word was God."* Our words, composed of our God-Self's subtle energies, automatically bring the meanings of our words into being.

As we contemplate this, we become aware of how much our attitudes towards our self and others affect how we feel physically and how our life takes shape. Both our bodies and our life situations perfectly reflect our thoughts and feelings, and are easily viewed by others via our body language.

Changing Your Conversation With Your God-Self

A recent newspaper article suggested that the newest, quickest way to feel better about yourself is through plastic surgery. "It's even replacing psychotropic drugs and psychotherapy," the article reported.

The "cut-and-paste" approach of plastic surgery may improve one's outer image for a while, but it does not produce authentic change. True transformation comes from within, and requires a complete change in the way one sees and speaks to oneself.

An effective first step in creating a "new you" is to let go of old judgments, superstitions, beliefs, fears and any previous negative self-evaluation.

Next is to rewrite your life story by choosing a new view of how you see life and deciding what you really want to feel now. Your belief in the new words you speak will be in direct proportion to your willingness to accept new ideas about yourself.

"How do I truly want to think of myself?" you might ask. The answer could be, "I'd like to think I'm a happy, productive, beautiful person, doing my best in the world."

Next, you might ask, "Could I allow myself to be that great?"

In response, you might be tempted to retreat to the old image of yourself, or, instead, you might courageously change your conversation with yourself: "I want to do and be what I'm most passionate about. It could be a lot of work, but I will see my work as an adventure, not a burden. I can and will re-define a whole new idea of myself."

You might even add, "I choose to be loving, inspiring, happy, joyful, and playful, using every part of me in the most magnificent and illuminating way. I choose to be conscious of my God-Self every day."

Having trust in the power of your own words will come with practice. Be your own scientist. Experiment and observe what happens. Choosing your thoughts is totally creative and can be lots of fun! Learn to write specific statements, clearly describing what you want for yourself. Start by making a list of everything you wish for. Decide that everything you want is possible.

People adept at manifesting their dreams tell us, "Visualize yourself winning in your life—being strong, courageous, and free."

The Power of Your Words

Exercise 13

1. Design what you want in your mind's eye. Purposely "boot out" any previous negative beliefs saying, "Go away. Be gone. I'm letting go of that 'old' thought, because it's not what I want to think now."
2. Focus on how you want the new creation to look and feel.
3. See yourself having, doing, or being it—visualize how you want to receive your request and see yourself as already having, doing, or being it.
4. Thank your God-Self for making it happen.

When you consciously choose, with conviction, your words come from a new place within. Trust that your words come from your powerful center of being and are in the process of taking form now.

Speaking About Yourself

Exercise 14

1. Recall the last time you made a comment about some aspect of yourself to a friend.
2. Was it a criticism or was it a positive comment about yourself?
3. Do you still want that statement to be true for you now? If your answer is "no," what thought could you choose to think instead?
4. Create a sentence out loud to yourself stating what you do want.
5. Notice how you feel inside now.
6. Can you allow yourself to believe this new thought as the truth of you now?
7. Can you allow it to be okay to feel this good about yourself?
8. Repeat this new thought to yourself every day and notice what you feel.

A Healing Consciousness

No two thoughts can occupy the same space. When you think a new thought, what happens to the old one? It's either let go or stored in your memory.

You can let go of a thought faster by replacing it with another you would rather think. You have a choice. One of the best ways to release a painful thought is to replace it with its opposite.

The challenge with this method is to accurately discover what the opposite of the thought is for you, personally.

Joey

Joey felt his friends had abandoned him. No one had called him to play baseball in a long time. He was sad and angry. He also assumed they didn't like him anymore. He asked himself, "What could be the opposite of feeling abandoned?"

What came up for him was, "I want to feel included and cared about by my friends."

Rather than backing away from his friends and continuing to expect they didn't like him, Joey decided to do the opposite—to both include himself and to care about his friends. He took charge and made phone calls to his pals.

Joey discovered they had been feeling the same way and were hoping someone would initiate a new game. The old feelings simply evaporated when the new, loving thought took its place.

Emmett Fox, the eminent theologian, calls the basis of all metaphysical healing, *the law of mental equivalents.* It is a process of erasing an existing thought by replacing it with an equally powerful thought in the direction you'd like to think. The *law of mental equivalents* requires that you have no leftover feelings attached to the old thought and are not storing it as a possibility or resentment.

Fox tells us that it takes three elements to produce a new object or condition: clarity of thought, imagining the feelings you will have when your desire manifests, and faith in your God-Self power to make it happen.

Faith is your trust in the "*unseen.*" It is your conviction and knowing that your individual God-Self and your Universal Self are inseparable, eternally.

My Hero, Patanjali

We use our minds to operate in the three-dimensional world, but the practice of meditation allows us to let go of thinking all together and rest the mind in a thought-free state of Divine awareness. In meditation we move beyond the mind and connect with our essence, our pure God-Self, which is Divine.

When we learn to meditate, we develop the skill to let go of thoughts, stop them, or change them. Through an uplifted consciousness we can transform negative low-energy thoughts and create new, uplifting realities.

Patanjali is my hero. He was a great meditation master and scientist who lived in India in the 2nd century BCE. He was the author of *The Yoga Sutras,* teachings of truth we can contemplate and apply to our everyday life. He taught that when we quiet the mind, the thought-waves in our minds subside and we experience union with God. The skill of meditation helps us transcend learned cultural programming and shift our focus to our God-Self. In meditation we feel ourselves *One* with God.

Patanjali researched human thinking processes in detail. He taught that with awareness it's possible to change the content, mood, and direction of our minds at will. He taught that most people spend 80% of their lives thinking thoughts that are complete fantasies that never really manifest. (Panic attacks are such catastrophic fantasies.)

Pantanjali taught students to observe their thoughts and differentiate between the types of thoughts they think, thereby gaining mastery over their minds and their lives.

He taught that when we are able to let the mind rest, we can actually experience total union of our individual self with God. When we can predictably quiet our thoughts, our mind becomes our great friend, and with this skill comes the ability to choose which thoughts we want to think and which we do not want to think. We can build a truly strong, able mind and life.

You may have meditated many times throughout your life, but you may not have known that what you experienced was meditation. Whenever we are completely focused on something, we find ourselves in a state of meditation.

When our goal in meditation is to feel God's presence, we notice that, when all our thoughts quiet down, we feel completely connected to our great, expanded God-Self.

Often in a state of meditation we feel greatly energized as well as in touch with our own omniscience, omnipresence and omnipotence.

Meditation

There's no place like home!

There's no place like home!

The state of meditation gives you the feeling you are truly *"home"*—enveloped in the state of love.

In the classic film, *The Wizard of Oz*, the heroine, Dorothy, is hurled away during a fierce Kansas tornado and stranded in a totally different dimension called Oz. She happily meets Glenda, the loveable Witch of the North, who acts as Dorothy's guide and tells her of the secret power in Dorothy's red shoes—her legacy from the Wicked Witch of the East who was killed when Dorothy and her farmhouse crash-landed on Oz.

On Oz, Dorothy encounters three characters who love her and accompany her to meet the Wizard of Oz: the Lion, the Tin Man, and the Scarecrow. Each hopes the Wizard will give him a special quality that will make him more powerful in life. The

Lion asks the Wizard for courage; the Tin Man asks for a heart; and the Scarecrow wants a brain.

Dorothy's request of the great Wizard is simply to empower her to return home.

The story is a wonderful metaphor for our own spiritual journey home. "Home" for one on a spiritual path is the feeling state of love. It is similar to what you feel when you recall a happy memory, greet an old friend, cuddle your child, or fall in love. "Home" is experienced in the present state of "now."

In many spiritual traditions the state of "home" is experienced in meditation. It is the experience of peace of mind, quiet, and sweetness. At other times it can be exhilarating and filled with titillating energy.

A saint experiences "home" as his natural everyday state of union with God, with ever-increasing magnitudes of ecstasy.

But most of us need a little assistance. In *The Wizard of Oz*, Dorothy's beloved guide, Glenda, reveals to Dorothy a secret ritual and a mantra to repeat that will help remind Dorothy of her goal and easily return her to her beloved Kansas and Auntie Em's and Uncle Henry's farm: "Click your heels three times and repeat, *'There's no place like home. There's no place like home.'*"

Back on Oz, the Wizard reveals to Dorothy that she has always had the power to return home but didn't know it.

In the final scene, The Wizard of Oz reassures the Lion, the Tin Man and the Scarecrow that they, too, already possess the qualities they were wishing for. They simply had not known those specific great and wonderful qualities already existed within them.

This is the story of each of our lives until we meet an enlightened teacher of the highest truth or have an experience that propels us *"Home,"* like Dorothy. The job of the spiritual teacher is to awaken the experience of God within us.

Until you begin to have the knowledge that God really is who you are, you can feel you're always searching—lost on Oz, so to speak. Returning "home" is an experience you may want to have often in your life until you feel "home" all the time. Then there is no difference between your waking state, your deep-sleep state, and what you experience in meditation.

Enlightened masters of meditation know, when you have the ability to quiet the mind, you have everything.

You've learned what meditation is about, now let's look at what makes the practice of meditation so profound.

The Power of Sound

When I was growing up, my bedroom was directly above my mother's grand piano. My mother would wake me up each morning with either a concerto, a waltz, a lullaby or a lively march. (Occasionally her "percussion instrument" was a vacuum cleaner.)

I could feel my mom's mood for the day by the piece of music she chose to play toward the end of her practice session.

My mother was a spiritual seeker herself. She would continually experiment with trying to change her thoughts. She would often say to me, "Carol, you don't have to hold onto that thought, you know. See what you can do to change your mind."

Sometimes she would try to achieve peace of mind through sound, specifically through music. I could always tell when she wanted to change a certain mood she was in, because midway through a piece she would simply stop and abruptly turn the page of music to a more bouncy or lively tune.

My mom had discovered on her own that sound, one of the five senses, could affect the state of her mind. She had learned that certain sounds make us feel anxious, while others calm us and help us feel peaceful and happy inside.

Sound itself is powerful. Some sounds wake us up, like the music of a marching band, whereas other sounds, like the rhythmic crashing of ocean waves, brings our attention deep inside.

In addition to being a spiritual seeker, my mother was a concert pianist and played the organ in a church in Michigan for many years. Her organ was positioned close to the minister's lectern, so she felt the impact of every word he spoke at each service.

My mother was generally a peaceful, loving person, but she told me that instead of coming away each Sunday morning feeling inspired and peaceful, she usually felt upset and agitated. She began to study the teachings of other spiritual traditions around the world and brought various books into the church service with her, hiding them on her lap as she played the organ.

Every once in a while the minister would look down on the congregation and say, *"You all are sinners. Repent now or you are going to hell."*

Mother told me, "I would look down on my lap and find a passage from the writings of a saint, such as, 'You are made in the image and likeness of God. You are always whole and perfect and made of pure light.' Those words themselves had such a great effect on me. Gradually I moved more toward teachings that resonated with my own inner harmony."

Mantra

A mantra is a word or phrase composed of sacred sound syllables and meanings that resonate with, and when given to a student by a true saint, is charged with the power to activate the process of Self-knowledge in the student. It is an instrument of sound that has developed a field of divine energy around it. A mantra given to you by an enlightened saint who is a true Guru, takes you to the most expanded state of peace and experience of God within yourself.

Knowledge of the power in mantras has been used for thousands of years to give people tools to quiet their mind, calm their body, and regulate their breathing.

Mantras are made of special sounds that consist of very pure vibrations. In all cultures and religions great seekers of truth have respected the pure creative power of those sound vibrations.

In the world there are myriad vibrations moving at different frequencies. All matter and even non-matter is composed of vibrating energy. The saints tell us that one reason some people experience more happiness and bliss than others is that their thoughts vibrate at higher, more loving frequencies. When you move your own thoughts to a more loving level of understanding, the associated vibrations and energy fields affect your body and your environment. You can actually feel the subtle shift of sensation in your body when that happens.

In David R. Hawkins' book, *Power vs. Force*, he describes how great beings, vibrating at very rapid frequencies, have the ability to transform the planet. Each of us has experienced how certain sounds calm us while other sounds energize us.

The same is true of words. Not only do spoken words consist of sound vibrations, they also have inherent spiritual and emotional effects. Certain words create higher vibrations than others. Some words can be of such low vibration as to feel sharp and painful, even when we don't know their meaning. We often can sense the meaning of a word simply by the feeling of the sound vibration it projects.

You can experience for yourself which words feel uncomfortable and which produce feelings of peace and love.

Mantras and rituals are happy vehicles to help us change our mental and emotional direction. The ritual of repeating a mantra over and over has many benefits. Saints offer their students mantras not only to help them calm their minds, but also to help them move from ordinary thoughts into spiritually contemplative states, shifting their attention to higher vibrations.

For centuries students of meditation have repeated the sacred primordial sound, "Om."

I like to think that the reason Om feels so "at home" is that the mantra is contained in the word, and whenever we say or think the word "home" we are inadvertently repeating "Om," which of course takes us to our one true home of unity with God.

"Om" is not only considered the original sound vibration of God. Om *is* God. In the Bible, John 1:1 says, "In the beginning was the Word, and the Word was with God, and the Word was God."

Try repeating the word "Om" in meditation. Find a comfortable, erect meditation posture and begin by repeating the mantra "Om" (pronounced "Aum") as you breathe in, and "Aum" as you breathe out. Gradually your mind will become quiet and take you to the peaceful contented feeling of "home." "Om" becomes a sanctuary, a refuge from your ordinary mind.

Eventually you will discover that you can take that feeling state of "home" out into the world into your interactions with others. This process of bringing the purity of your quiet mind out into the hubbub of everyday life is an important aspect of actualizing the saint within you. "Home" becomes the constant awareness of God within you as you experience your day. When you feel "home," you are continuously alert, conscious and ready for the task in front of you.

Mantras are given to students by their respective spiritual teachers or gurus to help the students release their attention from the ordinary aspects of everyday life. Repetition of mantras or prayers shifts one's focus from the material world and its needs, desires, emotions and pain to an awareness of the highest, purest state of unification with the Universal Self, one's God-Self.

In the Western Catholic tradition, parishioners recite the rosary as a way to focus on their chosen saint and bring their awareness to God. In the Eastern Christian tradition, both Orthodox and Catholic, the Jesus Prayer acknowledges the divine power that lies in the very name of Jesus.

Tibetan Buddhists repeat the sacred mantra *"Om Ah Hum Vajra Guru Padma Siddhi Hum."* With this mantra, one's ordinary mind quiets down and the pure awareness of one's *Buddha Nature*—the inner teacher—is revealed. The mantra enables the mind to transcend ordinary awareness and moves one into an experience of unity with God.

All Christians find that repeating The Lord's Prayer brings them similar feelings of oneness with God: "Our Father, which art in heaven, hallowed be thy name …."

Using The Breath As A Mantra

There is enormous power in our own breath. For one thing, we cannot exist in a physical body without it. Spirit and breath are intimately connected.

When a baby is born, the first thing it does is take a breath. For the next hundred-plus years, breathing does not cease until the moment when the breath leaves the body. When we learn to calm our breathing, our entire body becomes peaceful.

One of the most sacred mantras is the sound of one's own breath. The sound of the in-breath "Hum" and the sound of the out-breath "Sah" means, "I AM THAT, I am one with the Universal Self, I AM GOD."

In the practice of meditation, we learn to quiet the mind by focusing on our incoming and outgoing breath. The breath alone has the power to quiet the mind and take our attention to that peaceful place inside us. Focusing on the breath and simply observing its flow is the simplest way to calm our mind and regain our attention when we've been distracted.

The first step in learning to meditate is to establish a comfortable yet steady posture. The second step is to take in a long deep breath and let it out slowly and smoothly. Continue focusing on the breath as it comes in and goes out. This gives the mind a pure action and helps one's thoughts quiet down.

Those two steps alone will give you an immediate experience of the power you already possess to take charge of your mind.

The third step, while breathing slowly in and out, is to repeat a sacred mantra or your favorite prayer over and over. All sacred mantras are composed of vibrations of love. The mantra is that vibration of Divine Energy that draws you to your God-Self. That is why the saints tell us that you, the mantra, and the goal of the mantra—all are One.

Use The Breath to Calm the Mind

Exercise 15

This is a great exercise to use in the midst of any stressful moment throughout the day. At times when it's not possible to meditate, but you still want a quiet mind, use it to simply take charge of the depth and speed of your breath and it will help you quiet down.

With this exercise you will find yourself able to release tension, fearful or angry thoughts, and agitated energy, along with the physical discomfort created by such thoughts. You will find yourself experiencing a balanced and peaceful mind along with a relaxed and healthy body.

When your thoughts are going really fast, it's perfectly okay to talk to your mind and tell it, *"Stop!"* When you do that you are using a powerful tool called *thought-stopping.*

At other times you can be sweet to your mind and gently guide it toward harmony and peace. Know that a thought is only a thought and has no power unless you give it power. Use this exercise any time to calm your mind and regain your attention when you're distracted:

1. Find a safe and comfortable place to sit. With your eyes open, roll your shoulders back and let go of any tension you feel. Open your chest and take in a deep breath. Hold it for a few seconds, then release it, long and slowly.
2. Take in another deep breath. Hold it a few seconds, and again release it slowly. Now continue to do the same with normal-sized breaths. Hold each breath a few seconds and then slowly release it.
3. Notice how your whole body is slowing down and relaxing. When you feel comfortable, you can close your eyes and continue this process as long as you like.

Meditation—The Practice Itself

Exercise 16

Experiencing Being *Home*

Meditation is a tool to help you master every area of your life. The state of meditation is easiest to achieve when you set up a good time and place to begin. Begin spending ten minutes a day with the following meditation practice:

1. Find a comfortable and quiet space to sit. Creating a stable meditation posture is essential to being able to focus your attention inside. Sit in a comfortable upright posture with your legs either crossed in a sitting position or feet placed flat on the floor.
2. Place your hands gently on your thighs and close your eyes.
3. Take a deep breath in and a long slow breath out.
4. For five minutes watch your breath as it comes in and goes out.
5. Next add the phrase "I am That" as you breathe in and "I am That" as you breathe out. Continue repeating, "I am That" as you breathe in and again when you breathe out, until you feel love suffusing your whole being. When you feel that love you may let go of repeating the phrase and simply sit in the presence of your great, loving God-Self.
6. At first, meditate only as long as it takes to begin to feel peaceful. Each time you will meditate a little longer, having experienced the sweetness of the experience, and will naturally want more.

You may ask, "But what do I do with my 'monkey mind?'"

When your mind is scattered or when you notice thoughts coming up that you do not want, just gently bring your attention back to repeating "I am That, I am That." The mantra has many purposes, one of which is to help you redirect your monkey mind.

You are always more powerful than any thought you are thinking. Sometimes you feel you're being beaten up by a thought or a memory or even a worry about the future, but as you practice repeating the mantra and meditating, the feeling of being "Home" settles your mind and allows thoughts to simply float on by.

Like noticing clouds in the sky, you see that you don't have to hold onto them or resist them.

The Relationship of Sound Vibration to Matter

Saints of the ancient teachings of Kashmir Shaivism tell us of the sacred teachings of *The Tattvas*, the spectrum of thirty-six subtle categories of creation through sound. Study shows how the process of creation moves from the first five *Tattvas,* which constitute the pure creations, to the latter thirty-one, which form the impure creations.

The teachings tell us that the first step of creation was a thought impulse. That impulse took the form of a sound vibration that eventually transformed into a material form. *The Tattvas* show us how the spiritual teaching, "thoughts become things," works: Consciousness, in its pure form, first notices itself as "I am," and later as "I am that."

Then it identifies itself with more and more solid forms until finally reaching awareness in a human form: "I am a human being."

The process we know as evolution functions on this spectrum, from impulse to idea to matter, creating unlimited animate and inanimate forms and material objects.

In his book, *The Music of Life,* the Sufi Master Hazrat Inayat Khan tells us, "The impression of sound falls clearly on all objects, but it is not always visible."

Testing the effects of sounds under the microscope, scientists have observed that sounds can create clear impressions of leaves and flowers and other things of nature, proof of the belief held by ancient peoples that God, in its first step towards manifestation, was audible and in its next, visible.

These observations also suggest that everything we see in this objective world, every form, has been constructed by sound and is a phenomenon of sound.

Khan says that sound and breath are not different from one another. "The original condition of a word is breath. If we said, 'First was the breath,' it would be the same as saying, 'In the beginning was the Word.'"

The ancients taught that the breath and the soul are one. It is a kind of ethereal magnetism, a finer kind of electricity, the current of which goes in and comes out, putting the air into action.

Khan wrote, "Breath is the very soul of man. If there is any trace of the soul, it is to be found in the breath."

The Journey is One With the Goal.

D.T. Suzuki

Chapter 8

Navigating Life Now That I Know I'm God

I was seventeen, on my way to college, waving goodbye to my mother standing on the runway of Hawthorne Airport. I couldn't figure out why my mother was crying, because I was feeling wonderful—alive and free.

My dad was at the stick of his beloved Bonanza with an intent and happy smile on his face as we took off into the wind over the Pacific Ocean. He had decided to fly me to college himself instead of buying me a ticket on a regular airline. Flying was his passion. Dad would do anything to get a friend or family member to go up with him.

My dad was nineteen when he built his first airplane in the town park in Jackson, Michigan, the same time that Charles Lindberg was flying across the Atlantic Ocean to France. Dad had built a biplane, jet propulsion engines and brake systems during World War II and had taken apart and put back together *Charlie,* his Bonanza, a hundred times.

On this day we both felt liberated. We both felt totally alive. However, in the hours to follow, my dad would continue to be excited, but I would be scared to death. He knew how to navigate the airplane. I didn't.

A few hours into the flight, with the sky dark, I saw the plane headlights reflecting in huge cumulus clouds. Soon we were tossed violently up and down—the ground nowhere to be seen. The wings slid first to the right, then to the left. We bounced from cloud to cloud. A huge rainstorm somewhere between El Paso and Dallas had begun slashing at us through the atmosphere. I was terrified!

My dad kept watching the altimeter and those dials that describe whether or not the plane is steady on the horizon. The dial jumped and I jumped. I wished I could understand how those dials worked so that I could feel more in control.

My dad was flying by instruments, and was confident he knew where he was going and how to get there. As in life sometimes, I felt I was flying blind.

Several hours later, the wind behind us, and the sun shining brightly through the clouds, we gracefully and smoothly touched down at Love Field.

I never again doubted my dad's ability to pilot the skies, and I wanted to have just as much skill and conviction in piloting my life. I spent the next four decades taking "flying lessons" of different kinds, including life skills trainings of all kinds: relationship, meditation, communication, and healing-the-body skills.

Like you, I'll undoubtedly continue learning how to use my wings until I leave this life.

When my dad was ninety-three, he chose to die in his own bed in his own house in Southern California. I was concerned that his whole life had been about taking care of family and creating material things. I assumed he had not addressed the spiritual side of his nature.

Knowing that Christianity was the only religious orientation he had known, and eager to help, I asked him, "Dad, Is Jesus real to you?" I was hoping he was not afraid of passing on. I hoped that he believed in a power beyond this life. I thought if he did, he might feel calmer and more peaceful.

He paused for only a moment, looked at me earnestly with his big, fading blue eyes and replied, "No—Jesus is not real to me, but I believe that The Christ Spirit is within everyone."

I was elated. "He has done his work!" I thought to myself. My dad understood that "The Christ" is not only in Jesus, but is the power and energy of God that exists everywhere in everyone. My dad wasn't afraid to die.

He very peacefully let go of his body the next afternoon.

Using Your Own Inner Compass

In the same way that my dad used his instruments to navigate us through the sky, you have your very own instrument panel. It's your inner knowing. You can read it easily because it doesn't "dial up" fear, anxiety, or doubt. It reads as peaceful, confident assurance. That knowing is beyond thinking and beyond time and space. The compass you employ to navigate your life becomes easier and easier the more you use it and the more you know how to interpret what it's telling you.

Ask yourself, "Do I shift the screen of my consciousness to the widest, most expansive lenses, or do I take a reactive, short, narrow view of things? Do I let my immediate emotional grooves or habits dictate my response to things, or do I listen to my higher, inner knowing? Do I seek the highest truth of my God-Self?"

Please go to the place inside you where you talk with your God-Self. Go there often. Check your weather, and by all means correct your flight plan whenever your compass readings are off.

State of the Art of Flying

Just as some of you are beginning to understand, experience, and investigate the infinite, unlimited nature of your own being, researchers are engaged in parallel research in the unseen energy realms of science. What they are finding is turning past concepts of what is real upside down.

Many such scientists are discovering that what we've believed about the relationship of genetic, viral, or bacterial causes of biological conditions in the human body just may not be true. In the beginning of this twenty-first century, some are finding that the causes of illness may have more to do with the informational morphic field that surrounds a person or group than with genetics, viruses, or bacteria.

This new information points to the level of importance we each give to the beliefs and information we receive from our environment, and how much these influence our individual health. We tend to create conditions we believe.

Psychology has known for years about the significance of both "the placebo affect," and "anniversary reactions" to what we experience. Both demonstrate how our expectations have the power to create outcomes.

My grandmother lived to be one hundred five and a half, as I mentioned before. Did I tell you about how, when she was eighty-five, she and I were walking down California Street, one of the steepest of San Francisco's notorious major boulevards?

Nana was laughing and poking fun at "old people," pretending to use a cane and wobbling crookedly down the hill. "I'll never grow old. I'll never grow old like this," she said. "I like being with young people. They think differently!" she exclaimed.

At that time I thought to myself, "My Nana is being a comedian, cracking a cruel joke." I laughed with her. But in retrospect I know she always chose to spend time with young people.

"I don't like being with old people," she'd say, shaking her head.

What she meant of course was, "I don't like the attitudes—the emotional and thinking environments of old people. I don't like the (informational morphic fields) generally created by old people. I feel better when I assume the attitude of the young—their enthusiasm, hopefulness, excitement about the future, their interests, and trust in life, etc."

Seeing Your Life Itself as a Spiritual Practice

Living in the Light, Feeling the Light of Your God-Self

Mastering life requires love, understanding, and skills. Mastering life means attaining the knowledge of who you are, learning what infinite capacities you have, and then practicing and refining each of your powers and learning how to apply them in your life in the most loving and uplifting ways.

So far, you've learned you are in fact divine—God expressing as you in the universe. You've been introduced to the unlimited powers that exist within you, and even those you may not be aware of yet.

Next, you will learn practices that purify and strengthen your ability to use those powers. They are called "spiritual practices" because they each lead to the experience of divine energy within you, and then expand out from you into your environment and the world. You've had many experiences of your divinity already, but in this chapter you'll learn how to create and sustain them yourself.

Spiritual Practice Leads to An Evolution in Consciousness

Great feelings arise through spiritual practice. Sensations of bliss, peacefulness, love, happiness and creativity are some of the feelings that emanate from spiritual practices such as the repetition of God's name, meditation, or just simply thinking loving or compassionate thoughts.

Once you know you can have those delicious sensations and be in such a state of awareness, you'll want to go there frequently and maintain such great feelings throughout your life. Once you have the conviction that you are a ray of God, you'll want to live in that exquisite consciousness every day.

There are unlimited kinds of spiritual practices that take you to the experience of unity with your God-Self, but any action with a positive intention is a spiritual practice, and any kind thought or action is also a spiritual practice.

Students tell me they've had exquisite feelings of Oneness with nature, and with their children and beloved pets, and they want to have more.

Practice, Practice, Practice

A Ritual Is a Practice

Enlightened teachers tell us that practice is necessary to stabilize the awareness of our God-Self. Saints have given students rituals to help them feel the Presence of God within. In every culture, God-centered rituals have been integrated into seasonal and life-cycle transitions to ease the impact of change and to acknowledge celebrations of birth, growth, coming of age, marriage, education, completion of skill training and the assumption of responsibilities.

Rituals have also been used to mark the spiritual growth and development of an individual, family or community, and have been used to bring the awareness of God's Presence to an individual in the transition we call death.

Both modern and tribal communities around the world use rituals to organize their societies for all kinds of purposes—religious, cultural, survival, economic and educational.

God's Presence is especially felt in rituals where communities play music and sing and dance together. The dancing Sufi whirling dervish is a perfect example of how ritual provides seekers direct experience of God's love, power and energy.

Spending time in nature is also a great way to feel God's presence and achieve an immediate here-and-now focus. A teenaged boy told me, "I always see God in nature. I often feel inspired in the woods. I feel the rhythm of the rain, the energy of a tree, and the spirit of a friend and of all creation."

Many practices teach "selfless service," such as caring for others, or offering monetary gifts or other fruits of one's labor to the community.

Chanting the unlimited names of God is a special favorite of mine, because it's fun and puts me in a happy, joyous state of mind. I feel the ecstasy of God in the form of an inner nectar when I sing.

Saints honor the body as the temple of God and ask students to treat their bodies with enormous respect and love. They remind us to express gratitude to our body for all we receive. They teach us the importance of keeping the company of the truth.

A student asked his teacher, "What is our purpose here on earth?"

The teacher replied, "To glorify God."

"What does that mean?" the student asked.

"When you keep the company of the Truth you are practicing your highest God-Self. You are celebrating and honoring God in you. Love yourself, for God is who you are," replied his teacher.

When you are feeling derailed, a spiritual practice can help you get back on track.

Keeping good company is really important. Turn to the teachings of the great saints and re-establish their words in your heart.

Monitor yourself during the day. Notice if your vibration or energy has dropped. If so, bring your focus to something you love—something that feels honest and pure, happy and loving.

Rituals and practices help realign you with your great center of knowing. In every spiritual tradition, rituals have developed to bring people close to God.

Muslims pray five times a day, tuning in directly to the Divine Presence within them. They take time throughout their day to remind themselves of their relationship with God. In Buddhist and Hindu traditions, students sit for meditation with the goal of quieting their minds, communing with their highest Self, and experiencing the peaceful Divine Presence within them. In most Christian denominations, students are encouraged to pray and perform rituals that offer a direct experience of the Holy Spirit. They observe the communion rite, fast, and sing hymns. Jews practice chanting sacred prayers, contemplation, and reading sacred passages from the Torah.

There are unlimited methods for tuning into your God-Energy: meditation, prayer, contemplating spiritual teachings, chanting, self-inquiry, repetition of mantras, reading scriptures, helping others, offering physical and financial support, and keeping the company of a saint or others who support a loving orientation to life.

The most beneficial practice of all, however, is seeing God in yourself. When you notice you've been thrown off your emotional center by something—whether it's anxiety, fear, anger, frustration, pain, or grief—it's important to re-balance yourself as soon as you can.

A good first step is to take in a gentle, easy breath and exhale slowly. Continue to breathe slowly and smoothly while you use one or more of the "*shifters*" (practices) to help you regain your good feelings about yourself or another. You can also turn to a favorite teaching that helps remind you of your God-Self.

At minimum, you can distract yourself, change your mind, play music, sing your favorite song, or call a friend.

It's also possible to re-set your energy level by exercising or even taking a moment to drink a glass of water. Take a walk, ride your bicycle, walk up and down stairs, or jump up and down. These sound like funny things to do, but they are wonderful tools to use to shift your attention to your more peaceful, radiant God-Self.

Through rituals and practices we are spiritually propelled out of any upset or complacency and back into a rich, meaningful life. People who do not know the real purpose of rituals view them as obsolete. Because of their limited knowledge, such people see rituals as structures that separate us from each other rather than unite us.

In the early 1960s in America, many people left their spiritual communities because they felt the community members were hypocritical or too steeped in ritual. Many leaders of such churches, synagogues, temples and mosques unfortunately had not educated their congregations to the true purpose of ritual.

Those who know the true purpose of ritual believe that performing rituals is as essential as food. They use rituals to unite with their God-Self—their "Inner Guru." Rituals can shift our awareness away from the mundane aspects of life to our highest, divine nature.

A pilgrimage is a ritual of another kind. It is a sacred journey to the site of a shrine, synagogue, church or temple where a saint has performed sacred acts or prayers. The site is often filled with the spiritual energy of that saint.

Performing a pilgrimage reminds a student of the saint's spiritual gifts and the saint's personal connection with the divine. Often seekers on a pilgrimage report that the dust of their life events is washed away. Pilgrimages exist in all cultures with the purpose of helping to renew seekers' relationship with God.

Students of Islam dream of making a pilgrimage to Mecca, the holy site of Mohammad's teachings.

Each year, hundreds of thousands of Hindus visit the ancient city of Benares (Varanasi) to offer prayers in the sacred waters of the Ganges.

Both Christians and Jews travel to Jerusalem to honor Jesus and Abraham. Catholics make pilgrimages to the Vatican to experience the tomb of St. Peter.

A few years ago, I visited the Church of St. Francis in the little hillside village of Assisi, Italy. It's said that when a great being leaves his body, the Divine energy accumulated during his lifetime continues to provide healing.

St. Francis' tomb is located in the basement of the Church in Assisi. If you travel there yourself, you will feel his powerful, divine energy still present there.

This is true of the sites of other saints, too. Perhaps you have visited the healing baths at Lourdes, France, or felt the exquisite energy at the Tomb of the Unknown Soldier high in the hills of Kyoto. Have you ever meditated at the shrine of a great saint, or possibly at the gravesite of your own beloved spiritual teacher? In all spiritual traditions, pilgrims travel to the teaching centers of their saints in order to immerse themselves in the intoxicating spiritual energy of these great beings.

Spiritual retreats are a means for separating yourself from ordinary routines and absorbing yourself in God's Presence. Retreats nourish you and remind you of your true, divine identity.

Monitor yourself periodically. Notice if your energy has dropped. Even mild concern can bring your energy down. Don't get derailed. Ultimately, practices, rituals, pilgrimages and spiritual retreats are happy occasions that help you stay true to your own inner Self and inner purpose. They help you maintain your intention to stay attuned to your own divine God-Self.

Practicing the Virtues

The virtues are powers that support thinking and taking actions aligned with one's highest Self. They include courage, kindness, honesty, generosity, strength, trustworthiness, wisdom, humility, responsibility, adherence to one's values, and more.

In addition to the many rituals passed down from generation to generation is the virtue and practice of spiritual discipline. Mature human beings use some form of discipline every day to help them stay on purpose and refrain from becoming distracted.

Saints teach "spiritual discipline creates freedom."

What does that mean?

For me, it has to do with maintaining my intention to live in my highest or most virtuous God-Self. My intention takes form in various ways. When I make the effort to be aware of God residing everywhere—in everyone I meet, I feel freer to be with all kinds of people. I am not judging them—I find myself liking more people and not resisting what they can teach me. I feel freer to learn from them and to have fun with them. So the effort or discipline I use actually frees me from my own critical mind and bad feelings.

Since the goal of a beginning saint is to live twenty-four hours a day in the consciousness of his or her God-Self, the beginning saint disciplines his or her mind to look for the best in himself or herself and others.

That does not mean being a weakling or a co-dependent. The highly developed inner discipline of a saint discriminates between those thoughts and actions that are destructive and those that are beneficial and uplifting.

On My Way to the Ashram

I was taught the same kind of discrimination on a pilgrimage to India one year. Moments after my arrival at the Mumbai Airport, I located my bags and went to the long line of taxicab drivers outside the terminal. I asked each driver, "Do you speak English?" until I found a blonde-haired fellow who replied, "Yes." I fantasized that his father was of East Indian decent and his mother was Scandinavian or something like that.

I asked him if he knew the direction to the sacred site, and how many rupees it would cost to drive me there. He nodded that he knew the location, and I agreed to his price. With a big "yes," he took my bags and placed them in the trunk. Up until that point I was totally trusting.

I don't know how many of you have ever arrived at the Mumbai Airport at 2 a.m. in the morning, but if you have, you know the dark night is sprinkled with hundreds of small sidewalk fires and the sky is full of smoke. It was my introduction to India.

As we started out I held my breath and prayed. When I opened my eyes, I discovered that my taxi was speeding down the middle of a two-lane highway, trying to avoid a huge assortment of fires, donkeys, and oxen on each side of the road. Soon, I found myself gripping the seat behind the taxi driver "in case anything happened." Huge colorful trucks, painted with images of Shiva, barreled straight for us. I gasped!

Always at the last moment my taxi driver would swerve to the left. I was a California driver. I would have swerved to the right! I was still alive. A miracle! I was so grateful. It was one of those flashes of time when you know there's a God. There is not a wilder ride on the planet earth!

On that particular early morning, my driver really had no idea where he was going. It was actually illegal for him to drive customers outside of a specified area, so he paid off the policeman at the city checkpoint.

Needless to say, I was a captive. In order to maintain hope that I would arrive safely at my destination, I made small talk with the driver, who really couldn't speak a word of English other than "yes," and I fantasized how this fellow was a seeker of truth like me.

Not so! After six hours and unexpectedly having to pay for two full tanks of gasoline, I finally arrived at the Ashram. My taxi driver refused to let me have my bags unless I paid him more money.

Just then, a monk saw what was happening and came to my rescue carrying a big long stick. I wondered what the stick was for.

The monk started to hit the taxi driver really hard. I was aghast. Wasn't I coming to a place that emphasized love? The monk pounded on the taxi driver until he gave up my bags and drove off.

I was in shock! I tapped the monk's shoulder, "Please tell me what just happened," I pleaded. "I thought my job was to love him unconditionally."

He replied, "It has everything to do with love. That's why I hit him. If I do not provide him the consequences of his bad behavior now, he will experience it on his way home, possibly get into an accident and die.

"I don't want that to happen to that fellow, but it is absolutely not okay to allow someone to abuse you or steal from you."

That was my first lesson in "tough love."

The saints teach that we have more true freedom when we live life from the most virtuous perspective. That's why, like Moses and the *Ten Commandments,* the saints encourage honesty, love, compassion, generosity, justice, integrity, knowledge and wisdom.

Without the ability to discriminate, to restrain an impulsive action, word, deed or habit, we are simply puppets on a string, being jerked around, unfocused, seeking approval, unassertive, and ineffective.

Saints ask us, "If you are not disciplined, how can you trust yourself or be trusted?"

Other disciplines necessary to achieving freedom are truthfulness, the ability to make agreements and keep commitments, to live in moderation, to be steadfast, to have compassion, to be able to forgive and to persevere.

A skilled and disciplined mind is a prerequisite for achieving true freedom and power. Each person's mastery of his or her life depends on his or her ability to make disciplined choices aligned with his or her sacred duty as a ray of God. Such a person chooses "the high road"—the best, most beneficial, loving and wise action—in every situation.

The University of Life

The whole game of life becomes lots more fun when you see it as a marvelous adventure, spurring you on to greatness. When you take the point of view that each lesson, obstacle or challenge that comes up in your life is your own individual homework, designed to help you grow and flourish, you become more grateful for every day you live. Each obstacle presents another opportunity for learning and rediscovering the perfection of the God-Self in you and others.

Those of you who embrace your life lessons as spiritual opportunities choose to see every facet of life as a spiritual practice.

There are couples that use their marriage and family relationships as the basis of their spiritual practice. They see each challenge in their family as a gift through which to grow. They use their marriages as vehicles of transformation for both parties, honoring each other's individual paths and finding ways of coming together to share their learning, their excitement and growth. Their dreams and goals are created together. They learn to negotiate issues with generous hearts and an intention for both to win in life.

My husband and I often laughingly tell people, "We'll know when we're enlightened, 'cause then we'll be more patient with each other."

There are mothers and fathers who see parenting as their primary spiritual practice. Others focus on their careers. Students learn to use their education as their practice. But truly, each person's whole life offers lessons and teachings for unlimited spiritual growth.

While reading the following vignettes you may recall similar situations and how you handled them. Did you see your life situation as a problem or as a gift to learn from? Try to approach each of the stories as an opportunity to assess your own ability to maintain your peace of mind and congratulate yourself when you were able to accomplish it.

Life Lessons

Seeds

It took me eons to really understand the relationship between what I planted in my mind, and how those thoughts made me feel… until I met the saint who told me, "There are no innocent movies." She meant that the content of our life is the direct consequence of all the seeds we sow in our mind, what we see, what we read, what we think, the company we keep, and the attitudes we wear.

It was the shower scene in Alfred Hitchcock's movie *Psycho* that brought that teaching home to me personally. I'm still reeling from it. I only like to take showers when there are lots of people in the house. I wish I had never planted the images of that and other scenes in my mind.

Our Garden

One year, my husband and I planted a huge vegetable garden. Since we have many deer running free on our property, the first order of business was to build a strong, high fence. Our deer eat everything.

It took lots of hard work to build the plot, and finally it was ready for planting. We had proper fencing, proper soil, and organic compost. We anticipated the best-ever summer fare.

What actually happened? We harvested a total of one two-inch carrot!

Too late for that season we realized we had not provided adequate irrigation, and we had not counted on a family of rabbits tunneling under our brand-new fence. We were new to farming!

The experience made us hugely grateful for all the farmers in the world. We realized that to be successful in the future we'd have to educate ourselves, plan, persist, and be willing to correct.

Most of all, we could not give up. We could not let our ignorance, lack of knowledge of animals, or our meager skills stop us.

Our gardening experience was the perfect metaphor for learning what it takes to be successful in relationships, in life, and in our spiritual evolution. We learned we have to plant the best seeds, keep the weeds out, guard against our own inner scavengers, nurture abundantly, and be persistent in practicing the *Presence of God* in ourselves and in each other.

I've finally realized that literally everything that happens in my life provides me an opportunity to move higher in awareness.

So how do I know when life is presenting me with such an opportunity? I recognize it through my feelings. If I feel at all tense, angry, annoyed, or resentful, I know, OOPS! There's one of those lessons knocking on my head! "Wake up Carol," it says, "There's one of your hot buttons. What are you going to do about it? Can you see that button as a friend and grow from it?"

Sometimes I can see it. Sometimes I just choose to stew in the anger or pettiness for awhile, just because.... That's the truth. It's kind of like having a mud fight or a snowball fight, where you get down and dirty, or cold and wet, and you just enjoy the heck out of it ... for a few moments. Then you take a deep breath, a hot shower, change your clothes, and begin the day again.

That's how it is when I hit a hot button. I make a choice whether or not to roll around in the bad feelings for a few minutes, drop them altogether if I can, or shift my awareness to the truth using the "Beginning Saint Bridge," which I will teach you about in the next chapter.

Raccoons, Garbage and Gifts Story

John became enraged when he discovered that raccoons in his neighborhood had knocked over his trash cans—for the hundredth time—spreading shredded paper and garbage everywhere. Then he stopped himself and pondered, "How could

I see this incident as a gift? I know those raccoons are God in the form of raccoons, but …."

Reluctantly, he thought, "If I looked at what happened as a great gift, what could it be telling me? Let's see—I guess I could continue to be full of rage each time this happens, or I could laugh and clean it up over and over again. I could pretend that they are not raccoons, but that would be a lie. I could fantasize that they will all grow up and 'mature,' or I could be grateful they are raccoons, know that they have limited awareness of their God-Selves, and have compassion for them. Knowing all this, I could secure the trash cans in a more effective way. It's magical thinking to believe the raccoons will be other than raccoons in this lifetime."

John saw that God was playing each part perfectly in the unfolding drama of his life. He realized his expectations of raccoons were unrealistic, and finally found an ingenious way to secure the cans.

Now when he sees the raccoons peeking around the corner of his trash cans, he delights in knowing that God is showing up in the form of raccoons, and he just laughs.

Reminding Yourself of Your Greatness

Take a moment throughout your day to recognize your natural state of joy. If you're not feeling particularly peaceful, move to joy. Shift your thoughts. Use your mantra, meditation, music, or any uplifting ritual we've presented, to bring you back to your natural state of harmony, balance, and peace of mind.

You can do it, but you must find a way to love your own self. Remember your own inner-knowing instrument panel.

Ernest Holmes, the brilliant synthesizer of major spiritual traditions, presents reminders to guide your day:

1. Remember, God is everywhere. God is the only substance in the Universe. You are That, and you are made of love. You are eternal, unlimited, beauty, energy, creativity, health, and wisdom. You are that God that exists as you, in every breath, every thought and every thing. Feel God's presence in your own self.
2. Practice noticing God existing in all creations, and realize that you are made of that greatness. Think about this until you see that you are swimming in God. You live and breathe and exist within God, and God lives and breathes and enjoys life within you.
3. God is love. You are made of love. See love in your self. See love in each other. Know that everything is born of love. Feel the love you know you are.
4. God works through you. God works for you, through your own thoughts and actions. Because you were born with free will, you can choose to expand or limit what God does through you by limiting or expanding your own concepts of what is possible for you. You limit what God does for you through self-limiting beliefs in fear, lack, anger, and resentments. Give God a break. Set God free to dream even bigger dreams through you.
5. Learn how to change your focus and thereby change your life. Know that anything you could wish for is already yours. You are the one who opens your mind and imagination to what you have in your life, first, through your beliefs and then through your choices. Weed out any idea that keeps you from expressing your magnificent God-Self, and ask yourself, "Am I going to let that stop me?"

6. Open the door to receiving all that is possible. As you move your awareness to your true unlimited Self, all great things are revealed to you. As you operate more and more from this understanding, you feel your own greatness. Know, all qualities of God are mine, because I am a living ray of God.

Self-Inquiry Points the Way

Everyone contemplates, ponders, or wonders about something. When you design your next vacation, plan strategies at work, or think about where you want to place flowers in your garden, you are contemplating.

Self-inquiry, however, is reflecting on your own personal thoughts, feelings, and behaviors. One person may be more self-reflective than another. But even in witnessing or noticing your own thoughts and behaviors there comes a time in the process—a freeing point—where you let go of concerns regarding your personal self and allow your larger God-Self to reveal even greater awareness.

Scientists, engineers, designers, chefs and people in all other visioning fields use their power of contemplation—their inner knowing—to access breakthrough ideas. Contemplation is a tool used by all leaders, sages, and saints to help them rise above their ordinary understanding, habitual attitudes, and feelings.

A beginning saint practices emptying his or her mind and contemplating three major levels of awareness: the teachings of great beings, his or her own intuitive knowing, and his or her life lessons.

To contemplate these teachings requires taking time to sit quietly and purposefully explore questions.

Being willing to hear the answer is equally important. Your inner Guru or God-Self contains all knowledge. It is that aspect of your own self that is your inner teacher, lover, and best friend. As you contemplate a teaching and examine each facet of the teaching, your inner wisdom reveals truths to you. You will know they are accurate when you feel clear and peaceful inside.

Contemplation is a major challenge in practicing the Presence of God. It involves first quieting the mind and then focusing on a particular question you would like to understand better. Students often begin their meditation session each day by contemplating the words of a saint, such as: "If you wish to be successful, you must identify yourself with success."

Of course, as they strengthen their ability to meditate, they realize that they can also bring that skill out into their everyday lives. They look for answers that resonate with their highest understanding.

Often the truth startles us, bursting forth into our consciousness. In the 2008 primary elections for President of the United States, Senator Edward Kennedy endorsed the young Illinois Senator Barack Obama. During his speech, Senator Kennedy said, Barack could help to "heal America."

On hearing this I immediately started to cry. That's it! That's it! Senator Kennedy had accurately identified the huge healing shift in consciousness I needed to make in order to re-attune myself with what I know is the highest truth. I, like many Americans who had experienced the 1960s, had unconsciously been traumatized by feelings of hopelessness and despair ignited by the Kennedy, King assassinations and the tragedy of the Vietnam War.

From the perspective of life being "God's play," nothing is really out of order or really needs to be healed except our consciousness. But of course, most of us have a hard time viewing life that way as yet. It was interesting for me to observe in myself that I, too, had been harboring similar old beliefs of mistrust.

Barack Obama's message of reclaiming "hope," of expecting good, spoke to the yearnings of my highest Self.

Sometimes it's difficult for us to ever see the positive that can come from such tragedy. Exercise 17 will give you a new way to approach such painful events in life.

Seeing Your Life as a Spiritual Practice

Exercise 17

1. What positive things have I gained from kicking a habit?

   ____

2. What lesson did I learn from being rich or poor?

   ____

3. What spiritual challenges have come with my career?

   ____

4. What have I learned from losing a job, relationship, a competition?

   ____

5. What lesson resulted from a divorce, an illness, a disappointment?

   ____

Christ was able to claim to be the Son of God because he was aware of his inheritance. If you are aware of your divine inheritance, you too can claim your true self.

If you think that you are the son of your father, you can only claim to be the son of your father. But there are many different inheritances that come into the formation of your being, and if you are conscious of your divine inheritance, you can manifest it. This is a great secret.

-Hazrat Inayat Khan
The Music of Life

Chapter 9

Learning From the Great Ones

A true Guru is an enlightened saint whose goal is to awaken you to your own inner light, the light of your soul. In *Beginning Saint* we call that light your God-Self, the Divine Self that has always been present within you and will never leave you.

The word "Guru" means one who "brings light to darkness." A true Guru is a saint who embodies God so perfectly that in his or her presence you feel you are actually sitting with God.

The Great Ones focus their attention beyond what they see with their physical eyes. When you or I focus our awareness on a great saint—a being of light, we, too, can transcend limited states of mind. The understanding behind this phenomenon is that the Guru generates a level of vibration so intense that we can actually feel his or her presence, even when we simply think of the saint.

Students of the saints Sai Baba of Shirdi, Rama Krishna, Anandamayima and Paramahansa Yogananda reported feeling a palpable energy in the living physical presence of these great beings.

Today, even though none of these four saints are occupying a body at this time, their students say they experience the same undeniable energy when they simply focus their attention on the saint or contemplate the saint's teachings.

Some spiritual traditions call such spiritual energy "Shakti." In others it is called "Grace" or "Holy Spirit."

Students who visited the great saint Bhagawan Nityananda of India had many stories to tell about "Bade Baba," as they called him.

Bade Baba very rarely spoke a word, yet in his presence students experienced their lives change completely. At times when he did speak, Bade Baba gave his students succinct lessons such as, "Grace provides the shortest route and fastest way home to the place of our origin with the Infinite."

The teachings of great beings ring true with our God-Self, just as when we are with someone we admire we feel as though the person's light and energy fuses with our own and we experience great peace and oneness with him or her.

When you recognize greatness in someone, it's because the greatness within you resonates with that person's light.

The teachings of great beings are everywhere. They are found in each person we meet, in homes, libraries, bookstores, temples, mosques, churches and ashrams. They're on our bookshelves, in the drawers of every hotel, and on the Internet.

Really think about and consider the teachings of one of the following teachers. Notice if it resonates with your inner being. Notice if your own personal understanding is confirmed or deepened.

Contemplating the Teachings of Great Beings

Lord of all pots and pans and things ...
Make me a saint by getting meals,
And washing up the plates.

—Brother Lawrence

Ye Shall Know the Truth and the Truth
Shall Set You Free.

—John 8:32

The education of the will is the object
of our existence. Knowledge is the antidote
to fear.

—Ralph Waldo Emerson

Rebellious thoughts are like an abandoned
house taken over by robbers.

—Phadampa Sangye

This very earth is the Lotus Land of Purity,
And this body is the body of Buddha.

—Hakuin

The ever-perfect soul within will express itself more and more through every opening made possible by the right use of will and discriminative free choice.

The truly admirable are those who transmute adversity into a personal victory.

—Paramahansa Yogananda

Purity of Mind shows itself in a man's mood. The first sign of your becoming religious is that you become cheerful. What business have you with clouded faces? What right have you to carry this disease out into the world?

—Vivekananda

By denying the Atman within us, we deny it everywhere. Ignorance is false identification. It is misunderstanding one's real nature. Pure, eternal joy and peace are to be found only in union with the Atman.

—Patanjali

The Practice of Contemplation

Exercise 18

Steps to contemplating the teachings of great beings:

1. Choose a teaching above and read it out loud to yourself.
2. Sit with the feelings and thoughts it inspires within you.
3. Describe the feelings in words to yourself.
4. Ask yourself, "What does this teaching mean to me?"
5. Ask yourself, "Does it feel true to me?"
6. What feelings does it ignite? Turn the teaching upside down. Try to view it from several different perspectives.
7. Ask yourself, "What do I think the saint was trying to tell me personally?"
8. Close your eyes once again, if it helps you to concentrate. Let the teaching rest inside your consciousness for some time.
9. Ask your inner self, "All-knowing part of me, please tell me what I can learn from this teaching." Listen to your inner intuition, your inner heart. Allow the inspiration of the teaching to do its work.
10. What do you see? What do you feel? What did you learn?
11. How will you apply this new insight to your everyday life?
12. Create a section entitled "Life Lessons" in your own personal journal. Comment on your insights into this teaching.

13. Share your insights with a friend you recognize as a beginning saint, too. In this way the teaching becomes even more real for you.

Contemplating Your Own Life Lessons

The purpose of our birth is to achieve enlightenment. Some Great Ones say that between lifetimes we choose our bodies, our parents, and the major relationships and circumstances of our lives, in order to grow and evolve.

When we fail to ask the question, "What can I learn from this situation or person?" life can feel meaningless and punitive.

When we learn to recognize grace in our lives—the great gifts we are receiving—we find that our life lessons have been our greatest wealth. We come to see grace showing up everywhere—whether in good health and relationships, beauty, love and sunlight, or in storms and obstacles—all as opportunities to accept ourselves and the world as divine.

Perhaps you grew up without the support of a mother or father, extended family, or nurturing environment. What were you forced to learn? How strong a person has that made you? How has that experience made you the person you are today? What beliefs have you had about yourself because of your experience growing up?

Everyone on the planet has had situations, obstacles, or challenges that have acted as catalysts for their growth. For some, these catalysts have taken the form of relationship issues, addictions, difficulty with finances, impaired physical functioning, illness, bad political situations, educational limitations, isolation, trauma or experiences of betrayal.

Our job is to see that the Presence of God has also been in each of such events and to consider how each has contributed to, rather than limited, us.

Is it possible that everything does really happen for the best?

Contemplating and Learning From Your Life Lessons

Exercise 19

In order to contemplate, it's important to be in a quiet place free of distractions, to relax the body, and to take in a few deep breaths. If your mind is peaceful and your body relaxed, it will be easier to focus your attention inside.

Ask yourself all nine questions for each event that you recall.

1. What situation did I have, or do I have now, that I recognize is unresolved or still painful in my life?
2. Can I see this situation as a gift rather than as an obstacle or punishment?
3. What are all the things I've learned from this event, both positive and negative? Have I made a decision about it that will limit or free me?
4. What teaching of the great beings have I applied to this experience—forgiveness, generosity, compassion, gratefulness?
5. How have the things I've both experienced and learned, helped me to be the person I am now?
6. Would I have developed this ability without the experience?

7. Is there anything remaining in this event that's left over?
8. What would I have to think or believe in order to see it differently?
9. How can I apply my new awareness to my life?

Write down your new understanding of this situation in your journal. Take action, apply it, and share your new awareness with a friend.

Michael's Story

Michael had owned the only bookstore in town for the past twenty-five years. On New Year's Day, a huge flood demolished everything in the store below four feet from the floor.

When I asked him how he was doing, he replied, "Really, just great. The only thing I had to replace was the carpet that needed to be changed anyway. My landlord came over just after we finally shoveled out the last of the mud and told me that he wanted to buy me a new carpet so I could get back in business."

"It's a funny thing," he continued, "without the flood I might never have changed that ratty old carpet!"

The Lesson

Exercise: What was the lesson for you in Michael's story? How does it apply to you? How can you use it to see things from a higher perspective in your own life?

Rosie's Story

It was a hot day. Rosie was out in her back yard cleaning up weeds, thistles, and poison oak. Hidden in the weeds were pieces of broken beer bottles and debris left from her neighbor's construction projects.

One thought led to another and Rose found herself getting angrier and angrier, even contemplating revengeful thoughts—like throwing all the trash back onto her neighbor's property and getting the police involved. As she worked she found herself feeling worse and worse.

All of a sudden the phone rang. Rosie laid down her clippers, trash bags and gloves and flew to answer the phone. On the other end was an old friend inviting her to meet for coffee. The two made their plans and hung up.

After the call, Rosie felt a momentary impulse to return to her angry feelings, but stopped.

Instead, Rosie consciously made the choice not to return to her pre-call, self-inflicted misery. She chose to "let go" of her upset with her neighbor.

The tension she had been feeling dissipated, and she also realized she no longer felt the need to send a complaining letter to her neighbors.

Rosie contemplated how neighboring countries similarly get upset with one another. "I've got to start right at home," she told herself. "I think I will plan a neighborhood party with a happy intention, instead of complaining."

Rosie's change of mind created tremendous relief for her, and she decided to make peace start with her. She planned the party for the following weekend.

The Lesson

Exercise: What was the lesson for you in Rosie's story? How does it apply to your own life?

The Practice of Love

Buddhists, Christians, Jews and Muslims alike have taught that our most powerful enemies are the thoughts and emotions that sabotage our greatest aspirations. The path to mastery over such enemies is the path of love. Our health in all areas—physical, emotional, financial, political, relational and educational—is healed when we open "stuck" flows of communication and energy through loving forgiveness.

The inner discipline of love creates unlimited solutions, because God in us always knows what to do. Joy, forgiveness, kindness and generosity stimulate healthy flows of energy and peace, both emotionally and physically. A beginning saint chooses to see from this highest perspective.

Stuck Flows and Superstitions Reminder

Exercise 20

1. Notice if you have any limiting thoughts or superstitions about your own capabilities, relationship to money, education, age, health, creativity, personality, gender or ethnic background.
2. Identify each separately and with each ask yourself the following question: "Am I willing to release this self-limiting idea and remind myself that God

is everywhere, working perfectly within me right now?"

3. Let go of the old belief with a sense of humor. Say, "Thank you, dear old decision, you served me well, but that's enough. I'm letting you go now. I'm choosing a newer, freer idea of me.
4. "I'm choosing to see myself as capable and free in every area of my life."

Practice Living as God Lives, Thinking As God Thinks, Loving As God Loves

Love takes up residence in your entire life when you're able to see God in yourself and others. Abundance itself grows as you start to practice your new vision of yourself. You see through the eyes and knowing of an abundant person, and appreciate the gifts in everyone and in everything that happens. The Great Presence is always right where you are.

Are you choosing to feel close or distant?

Everyone manifests his or her highest and purest God-Self to the level of his or her understanding. As your experience of your God-Self grows, your true abilities will be revealed more and more. Your trust in your God-Self will grow, too. You will know with certainty, "I can have whatever I truly believe I can have. It already exists in my mind—the mind of my God-Self—and is ready to manifest in form."

You can purposely reclaim the truth of your life. You can choose the course you wish to travel, and also the destination you wish to achieve.

When a thought or belief surfaces that opposes your desire in any way, speak to it and tell it to go away. Choose what you want instead. Imagine writing that thought on a blackboard. Then, erase any part of the thought that is not a characteristic of you as a ray of God. In your mind, draw a picture of what you dream of. Now, see yourself having whatever it is. Imagine how you feel having, doing, or being that.

Express to your highest Self—your God-Self—your appreciation for all your new gifts. Feel your Great Self.

The Practice of Unconditional Love

Exercise 21

1. Recall a person in your own life who offered you unconditional love. Was it a parent, grandparent, neighbor, or perhaps a teacher?
2. Recall an unconditional love relationship you had with an animal. Was it with your dog, cat, or iguana, rabbit, snake or turtle?
3. As you remember the relationship, feel the person or animal's love for you. It may be hard to differentiate your love of them from their love of you. Love between hearts has no boundaries.
4. Is there anyone in your life today that you would be willing to love unconditionally? Consider even someone who might not return that love in the way you would like.
5. Can you love them forever, even if that love is not returned?
6. Notice how you feel inside when you contemplate unconditional love.

Be Your Own Hero

As a beginning saint, you embody the laboratory for life. Use your own life to experiment, challenge, and explore your own personal experiences.

Eventually you will achieve the twenty-four-hour-a-day shift in awareness that comes when every thought and action emanates from your highest God-Self. Gradually you will trust yourself, and instead of feeling separate from God, you will feel yourself merged in unity.

Anger will transform into compassion. Desire will transform into non-attachment, and isolation to inclusion.

You'll feel happy for others when they receive great things. Instead of feeling the kind of passion that throws you off-center, you will feel the exquisite passion of a balanced, harmonious and peaceful life. You will lovingly see God in yourself and in the world and accept all as it is.

You are truly free when you're able to choose your responses without reactivity. That is what makes a saint a saint. You become your own hero. You look at your life and see what you are thinking, because what shows up is a mirror of your consciousness.

Notice the state of your relationships with your body, your friends, your finances, your work, your children, your environment and your emotions. As you shape up your mind, you will shape up your life.

Know that God has always been working within you. You are the evidence that God is on Earth. If you are creating "small," notice that you have been thinking small. If you choose to create big in life, start choosing "big"—big thoughts and big, expansive creations.

You have the power within you to answer your own questions. You are the embodiment of knowledge, and practice will allow you to see your perfection.

Your Intentions Propel Your Future

An intention is a thought propelled towards a goal. It has the intrinsic conviction within it to energize the thought forward into a tangible creation.

The way it works is this: An intention will manifest and take a form unless there are counter or competing desires blocking its movement forward. Positive intentions take you where you want to go.

A negative intention is still an intention, but it is a thought creating a barrier to getting what you really want. Counter, competing, and dual intentions often sabotage your basic goal, making a clear flow impossible.

The power of intention, when it is clear, is unbeatable.

I Can Do It!

I Will Do It! I Am Doing It!

I Won't Be Stopped!

Here I Go!

Franni asked, "How do I stay focused on my intention?" I replied, "Fran, you know how better than anyone I know. Set a limit on your thoughts and don't allow any other thought or behavior to get in your way. As soon as you allow your mind some room to sabotage you, you've allowed a counter-intention to materialize. It's still possible to correct your course, but it will take a lot more time and skill. You have to set some limits with your mind."

Franni's goal was to run the San Francisco Marathon, but she had never run a marathon before and wasn't sure a sixty-year-old grandmother could actually do it. On the other hand, I had known Franni since she was eight years old, and she had never given up on anything. Even if she got bruised along the way, she had never let a doubtful thought keep her from doing what she set out to do.

Franni didn't win, but it was her first-ever San Francisco Marathon and she finished in a totally respectable time. She was even happy with herself. Franni's friends and family know her very well and trusted all along that she would do it. They know she always comes through with whatever she intends to make happen.

My friend Dave Lent teaches a workshop called, The 5 Keys to Mastery: 1) Discover your passion, 2) Find a guide, 3) Visualize the outcome, 4) Practice, practice, practice, 5) Play the edge from one's intention. He says, "Mastery of life requires maintaining our intention."

Sailing is also a wonderful metaphor for intention. When you sail, you have to adjust the sails constantly to be able to catch the wind. You don't say to yourself, "I've set my course now and I don't have to correct or learn from anything." Sailing teaches you to stay balanced and safe, but with your eye on your destination. In fact, the very same dynamic happens in football, basketball, baseball, hockey … and on and on.

Intention is a form of self-strategy. First, ask yourself, "What thoughts and behaviors are necessary in order for me to achieve my goal?" Then write them down on a piece of paper to remind yourself, "What do I need to think and what actions do I need to take in order to stay on my own purpose?"

Establish both your physical environment and the mental environment of your thoughts, so, like Franni, you can't help but arrive at your destination. It is a form of internal business plan. You evaluate all the dimensions of your intention, and by *keeping your eye on the ball*, the results happen automatically.

It's like that for beginning saints. They maintain their intention to grow, to know God, and to practice living in the awareness of their highest Self. They experience the kind of unity where their intentions, their God-Self, and their goals are inseparable.

Creating an Intention

Exercise 22

1. Think of something you want to have, do or be.

   ____

2. Contemplate what it would look like and feel like when it happens.

   ____

3. Notice how much conviction is in your intention. Notice how it supports you having, doing or being what you want. How does it feel?

   ____

4. What thoughts do you usually use to sidetrack yourself? Write them down on a piece of paper and then throw the paper in a wastebasket.

   ____

5. Acknowledge yourself for being true to yourself. What did you do specifically?

    ____

6. Feel the joy that comes with creating, doing and accomplishing your intention.

Conflicting Intentions

You ask, "What if what I want doesn't happen?"

If this happens, it may be due to conflicting intentions or to an aspect of your original intention that's unclear. A conflicting intention usually involves having another simultaneous desire that in some way opposes your original intention. It's always good to make sure your intentions are sparklingly clear.

On the other hand, if you have found your desire not showing up, it may be because the timing wasn't perfect yet, or you haven't taken responsibility for doing your part, or even that a more wonderful creation than what you intended is on its way.

How many times have you wished for something that did come true, and then realized later you didn't really want it after all, or you didn't want the unexpected consequences that came with receiving your desire?

People ask for fame and get fame, but they also get the irritations that come with fame: They get the bills, the unwanted attention, the incessant requests for favors, the lack of anonymity, the demands on their time, the loss of safety, and more.

Often we don't consider all the consequences of our desires—that's why it's important to clarify every aspect of our dreams.

Peaches and Cream

A client we shall call "Suzie" prayed for a "youthful complexion." Within a short time she actually manifested the youthful complexion she dreamed of all right … along with the acne that came with it!

Needless to say, Suzy "went back to the drawing board" and re-designed her intention as the following: "I have beautiful skin, and a clear, healthy and youthful-looking face."

A modern day saint reminds us, "You are the cook of the cookies you bake. You place the ingredients in the bowl."

Over the centuries, great saints have tried to protect humans from their own painful choices by presenting them with social guidelines—teachings that give people a framework for orderly social behavior, but those guidelines have not always been aligned with Universal Truth.

Those of us still observing misaligned rules we learned from our childhood spiritual traditions may need new lenses in our glasses.

Ask yourself, "Which laws and commandments are still beneficial to me now? Which are no longer valid? Why?"

Recognize that when things don't go your way, you can attribute your experience to a choice or choices you have made. Revisit the original purpose for a guideline you might be applying to the situation and ask yourself whether or not it is true to you from the perspective of your God-Self now.

My Aunt Henrietta and Tom, the love of her life, lived within a mile of each other for fifty years, but felt they could not marry, and never did. They had been told by their respective priest and minister, "Catholics shouldn't marry Protestants," and, "Protestants shouldn't marry Catholics."

Fortunately, not all of us are bound by such strictures in the twenty-first century, but similar social, cultural, racial and religious "guidelines" still operate in many cultures across the world.

Notice if you are bound by an outdated belief? How do you want to change it?

Counter-intentions

Creating Your Dreams: A Gigantic House

A dear friend, Sally, prayed for a "gigantic house in a wonderful neighborhood." She had dreamed of this house and had plotted how she would pay for it for years.

Then one day she actually saw the house on a street she had never visited before. There was a "For Sale" sign staked in the front yard. Sally was thrilled—the house of her dreams actually existed!

She told me the story of discovering this wonderful house, and of how excited she was dreaming of how she would decorate each room.

"So when do you move in?" I asked.

"Oh, I decided not to buy it after all," she responded.

"Why not?" I asked.

"I decided it would be too much work to clean," she replied.

I laughed, "If you could ask for the house of your dreams, don't you think you could also ask for the perfect housekeeper?"

Even though we know we have the ability in our own unconscious to create the life we most deeply want, we can also have competing counter-intentions that sabotage that vision.

Procrastination is one example of a competing counter-intention that takes us in a different direction, or delays the completion of a desire.

Sometimes a doubt, a worry, a sense of wrong timing or lack of integrity will interfere with the completion of an intention.

Sometimes we want a thing to happen, but also know that if we choose that thing we are not being true to our own highest good or to the highest good of all concerned.

We could probably make a list of hundreds of ways that counter-intentions sabotage intentions.

If, however, we develop awareness of how our actions are countering our intentions, we will start to sense when we're off-track or off-purpose. If we don't, our counter-intentions may stay totally out of our awareness.

One strategy for correcting intentions is to pay attention to our bodily sensations. Usually our chest or stomach will tell us when we're off purpose. Once we get clear about our intentions, however, the tension will release and we will experience a feeling of calm and peace.

When we identify our counter-intentions and redesign them so they accurately express what we want, we see our real desires rapidly manifesting before our eyes.

Identifying Your Counter-intentions

Exercise 23

1. Picture yourself already having or doing the thing you want.
2. Ask yourself, "What's the first thought that comes up when I think of really having it?" Is there any opposing thought or behavior? If "no," continue writing your intention. If "yes," go to No. 3.

____

3. Notice the thought or behavior. What is it? Does the thought limit you in any way from having what you say you want? If the answer is "no," proceed to No. 5.

   ____

4. What do you want instead?

   ____

5. Can you allow yourself to have what you desire? If not, ask yourself what you are willing to have instead. What correction do you need to make in order for your intention to manifest?

   ____

6. Do you still intend to have it, do it, or be it?

   ____

7. During the next week, notice how your intention is unfolding.

I Create Everything I Experience in My World

What a concept! This teaching was a hard one for Judy to grasp. She felt totally rejected by a group of people who were important to her. She thought that people liked her and that she "fit in," but she was told she did not belong.

Judy had no idea what she was thinking and doing to cause this rejection. She felt really hurt by the group and tried to understand why she wasn't included in their meetings. At first she couldn't see "her part in the play."

We talked about dual intentions, what she felt, and how she expressed herself in the group. She was willing to take an honest look at her behavior, and saw that she had wanted the group's approval, but had not been willing to perform to their expectations.

Judy realized she frequently felt angry toward, judgmental of, and disappointed with, group members.

She admitted, "I really tried to change what I considered dysfunctional communication patterns in the organization, but became unhappy when my contributions were rebuked. I recognize now my own pattern of judging and challenging authority. I did not wholeheartedly support the organization just the way it was. I understand now that my own desires were simply different from theirs, and I see how my dual intentions were sabotaging me."

Judy concluded, "I'm amazed how life actually does mirror my own thoughts and attitudes. Next time I get involved with a group I'll make sure my own intentions are very clear first."

Dual Intentions

Exercise 24

Regarding a relationship, a group, or a job, ask yourself the following questions:

1. Do we have the same objectives and values? What are they, and how do my own personal objectives fit in?

   ____

2. Are there ways that I can contribute?

   ____

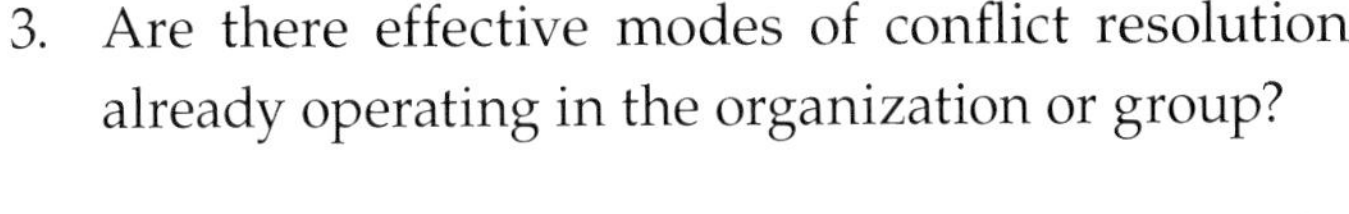

3. Are there effective modes of conflict resolution already operating in the organization or group?

    ____

4. Can I support the leadership of this relationship, group, or company?

    ____

5. Do I feel supported by this relationship, and do I receive enough benefit from it to be of value to me personally?

    ____

6. Can I be true to myself while involved in this group or organization?

    ____

If you can answer "yes" to 75% of these questions, and the remaining 25% do not sabotage your essential values and goals, continue to participate.

If, however, you cannot willingly support the relationship and you find yourself developing negative attitudes, either change your own mind or find a group you can wholeheartedly support.

Learn to Identify Your Competing Intentions

Saints who teach us how to meditate, give us the skills to be free of old beliefs and habits. They instruct us, via meditation, how to erase lifetimes of painful experiences. They give us tools that help us discriminate between one intention and another, between competing intentions, dual intentions, and conflicting intentions.

They teach that a competing intention is a thought or action that is an obstacle to and competes with your original intention. Often it is composed of underlying beliefs about yourself, such as "I want to be with this great guy, but I don't deserve to have a great guy in my life," or other thoughts that oppose what you want.

Sometimes limiting thoughts have been programmed in by the culture at large. Notice and let go of thoughts such as, "I'm not thin enough, rich enough, smart enough, young enough," or thoughts such as, "People like me can't do that."

Don't go into agreement with limitation. Tell yourself, "So what, I love me exactly the way I am. I'm God, for goodness sake!"

Contingency Thinking

A contingency thought says, "If I want this, then that has to happen first." We create a belief system for ourselves that binds us and won't allow us to achieve certain things before other factors are met.

In some families there is an unwritten rule that a younger daughter can't marry before an older daughter. In some, there's an unwritten rule that a son should play down his own accomplishments to keep from upstaging his dad.

Contingency beliefs abound: "I can't be happy until I'm married." "I can't have fun until I finish this project." "I can't spend money on myself if my child needs something." "I can't have a baby until I have forty thousand dollars in the bank."

This is "stuck," linear thinking. Notice how free you feel when you imagine just having, being, or doing without always considering "first things first."

Saving and planning are positive actions in life, but done in excess, they can be punitive and originate from fear. Contingency thinking can be a form of limitation. Your natural abundance comes from the recognition of the unlimited creativity of your God-Self.

Creating Your Dreams

Exercise 25

1. Sit quietly with your eyes closed. Gently take in a slow, even breath. Then exhale long and slowly.
2. Contemplate a question you want your God-Self to answer.
3. Write it down on a piece of paper before you go to bed at night. (Have some paper and a pen within reach.)
4. Place the paper with the question written on it on your nightstand or close by your bed.
5. Ask your question again silently to yourself before going to sleep.
6. When you wake in the morning, write down the answers that came up for you.
7. What answers, insights or direction did you receive?

Contemplating the Opposite

There are many strategies both psychologists and spiritual advisors offer students to help them change their thoughts. The saint Patanjali was one of the earliest known masters of the mind who taught methods for transforming habitual thought patterns. One of my favorite teachings of Patanjali is: When you don't like something, "*contemplate its opposite.*"

He taught that you have the ability to change your thoughts, feelings—and ultimately your life circumstances—by contemplating the opposite of the thought you are thinking and replacing it with one you want instead.

A Brand-New Year, A Brand-New Life

It was New Year's Eve when I first had the opportunity to test how *contemplating the opposite* works. I was still feeling lots of resentment toward my ex-husband for leaving me and not paying child support. It was nearly midnight and I did not want to drag any past bad feelings into yet another year.

I asked myself, "What am I really still upset about? Was it his leaving me for another woman?"

Well, I know that people change, and maybe he really didn't want to be with me anymore. I was sad that I was not the love of his life, but I could forgive him for being attracted to another woman. After all, I have lots of women friends that I love as people, too.

But I had not forgiven him for failing to financially support our children.

I asked myself, *"What is truly the opposite of failure to contribute child support?"*

I figured he owed me two hundred thousand dollars, counting half of two college educations and more.

As I contemplated, I recognized that the opposite of his *failure to contribute,* would be *for me to give something incredibly valuable* to him, instead.

As soon as I identified for myself what the opposite was, I needed to accurately identify what I wanted to give to him. "Should I give him money? Certainly not," I thought. "That would only make me feel more resentful."

I checked in with my God-Self. It told me, *"Offer him the most valuable things in the world to you."*

I had already given him his two adoring daughters and introduced him to my beloved spiritual teacher. Besides those precious gifts, the most beautiful physical gift I had ever seen in my life was a hundred-year-old family of bonsai redwood trees, offered to a friend on his forty-second birthday.

But my ex-husband was a landscape specialist and had thousand of trees in his life, so I decided not to give him a tree.

I had just completed reading *The Tibetan Book of Living and Dying* by Sogyal Rinpoche. It was one of the most important books I had ever read, and I realized my "ex" would like it too.

My heart started to sing as I thought about the great teachings he would learn. I was thrilled to find a gift that I would truly want him to have—one so filled with love, richness, and beauty that it would genuinely embody the opposite intentions of my pettiness.

When I recognized what the opposite really was, I felt a tangible release in my body. I experienced how a generous and loving heart could actually dissolve resentment. In the giving process I re-experienced wonderful feelings of love for him.

I decided to buy the book and send it to him as soon as the bookstore opened in the New Year.

It was New Year's Eve, five minutes to midnight, and all I felt was this incredible gratefulness and huge feelings of love. It was one of the most important lessons of my life.

Contemplating the Opposite

Exercise 26

1. For a moment, recall a limiting thought you have had about yourself. What is the opposite of that thought now? If you said, *I can't* do something, notice the physical feelings created by those words.
2. Now imagine *I can* and say to yourself, "I can do that," or "I can have that." Notice your feelings now. What happened?
3. Bring to mind someone with whom you have a resentment, someone with whom you've already tried to communicate, but the issue is still unresolved.
4. Observe any constriction or flow of energy in your body. Notice how your stomach feels and the amount of tension in your neck and shoulders.
5. Now take in a few slow, even breaths.
6. What is the opposite thought or feeling you could have for this person? What is actually the opposite of what you think about them? (Being accurate can sometimes be a challenge.)
7. You will know when you *have it* by the inner emotional shift that takes place. You will feel a huge sense of release and freedom.

8. If your new thought requires actually taking a positive action such as offering a gift or helping someone, then put it on your calendar and do it. You will feel even better when the action is completed or the letter is in the mailbox.

Attitudes Are States of Mind

A beginning saint practices the attitude of abundance, and finds that his or her "inheritance" is his or her state of mind.

The following story illustrates how thoughts create your destiny. Contemplate how this story relates to your own life and how you will apply it.

The Secret of Abundance

There were three families living in the same city. One family had inherited millions of dollars, property, businesses and fame. The family members were generous and kind and taught their children to respect themselves and expect the best of themselves and others. All of the members of this family expected abundance. When they lost money, they always believed they would be able to have it again, and they did. They all thrived. Money, beauty and riches of all kinds followed them wherever they went. They expected the best in their lives.

The second family also inherited generations of wealth; however the parents passed on their fear of loss to their children. Believing that they could lose their possessions, they hoarded what wealth they had inherited. Their children were not generous and behaved dishonorably. They did not contribute to others and invested unwisely because of their lack of trust. Family members slid into a gradual financial downslide into bankruptcy.

The third family was new to the United States. They came from a family history of poverty, but the parents believed that they could have everything if they worked for it. They believed that God was with them, guiding their every move. They trusted themselves and their new country. They trusted the people around them, and they taught their children that they could trust life. With belief in themselves, belief in God's guidance, inner conviction and wisdom, they lived abundant lives far beyond their expectations.

The three families embodied different attitudes toward money, different attitudes towards their abilities and the abilities of others. Each family's beliefs and choices produced the consequences they expected.

What do you expect? You are your beliefs. Do you want to change them? In which ways?

Learning How to Be Happy

My daughter Joie was starting the first grade at a new school when she came home one day and cried, "I hate school! Nobody likes me!"

On hearing this, I thought to myself, "How can Joie see God in herself and the other kids at school if her experience is so painful? How can I as a mother create an empowering experience for Joie that teaches her how the world works?"

Cognitive behavioral therapy to the rescue!

I thought, "If I can offer Joie this 'little' understanding, she might feel happier at school."

I asked her if she wanted to play a game. She was immediately engaged.

I explained to her that the game went like this, "Next week I will give you a gold star to put on your bulletin board every time you do something kind for someone at school. You can tell me about it when you get home. If you receive a total of twenty stars by the end of the week, I will take you to your favorite park to play."

Joie liked the idea.

At first I wondered if I might be manipulating my daughter with this game, but I also knew that if she learned how to turn her feelings around quickly, she wouldn't have to have years of painful experiences and come to conclusions about herself that were not true.

The first day of the game, Joie came home from school with a big smile on her face, "Mommy, I helped two people today at school."

"How did you do that?" I asked.

"I pushed Suzy on the swing, and I helped tie Johnny's shoelaces."

We placed two gold stars on her chart.

The second day she gleefully ran home. "Mom, I get fifteen stars today!"

"You do?" I replied. "How did you earn fifteen stars?"

She proceeded to tell me. She was so excited with herself, so joyful about school, and she had achieved this on her own.

The next day was the same. She learned that when she gave to others, the world gave back to her. She also discovered that when she was kind to others, she felt good about herself.

To tell you the truth, I don't remember which park we went to, but for the next eleven years I never heard her complain about kids or school again.

When parents come to me and ask me how to help their child make friends at school, I relate this story and ask them to help their child find ways of giving or sharing with their classmates.

They might share a story, perform a task together, or do almost anything that helps their child feel empowered and happy with him or herself.

The Cause of Depression

I was at a lecture with hundreds of people several years ago when the master of ceremonies asked the audience, "What is the cause of depression?"

I was a therapist already and thought, "I'll give someone else a chance to answer the question."

But of course I answered the question to myself—the same answer I had heard and experienced many times in the past: "Depression is anger focused inward."

One person after another offered suggestions. To each one, the master of ceremonies responded, "Wrong!"

Finally, he said, *"The cause of depression is lack of gratefulness."*

I was stunned. How does gratefulness have anything to do with depression? I considered the question for some time.

The speaker continued, "Lack of gratefulness can become a general attitude toward life. If prolonged, it can eventually limit one's ability to see and experience beauty, love, kindness, and generosity."

"Practice being grateful for everything," he counseled, "even those things that make you upset. Try to find the gift in the event. It is a great opportunity to grow."

Gratefulness

Take a look at the following areas of your life: Ask yourself, "In what ways am I grateful for my life, my body, my family, my friends, my health, my home, my job, my finances, my community, my country, my world?"

Notice what you feel when you think grateful thoughts. There's a song that says, "Bring back that lovin' feeling."

When you hit a dry period in your day or your life and you want to reconnect with love, practicing gratefulness is a surefire way to get you there.

A Stuck Decision Keeps Everybody Stuck

Alice was fifty-one years old when she realized she was still holding on to an old grudge against her stepmother. Over the years, Alice had tried to forgive her stepmother, but her underlying judgments permeated the atmosphere between them for years.

One day her stepmother courageously approached Alice and asked, "Alice, when are you going to forgive me? How long will you make me pay for the mistake I made when I was nineteen?"

Alice broke down in tears, "I've wanted to turn my feelings around for decades, but I didn't know how."

As a beginning saint, Alice knew she had kept her relationship with her stepmother stuck in anger. She recalled the many years of awkward meetings, the tension and the pain she had held onto.

In a single moment she made a new choice—to connect with her own God-Self and that of her stepmother. She was able to let the animosity completely release and transform into forgiveness and compassion.

How does this apply to your own relationships? How many friends or family members, bosses or co-workers have you "written off" over the years?

What if you forgave them?

Keeping good company is important for staying healthy yourself, but holding grudges sits in your body.

Why not let go of old, stuck decisions? See God in that person. Create a new life in this way now.

Changing a Decision

Exercise 27

1. Recall a decision you've made about another that's not accurate today.
2. Stop. Ask yourself, "Do I want the feelings that come with that old decision? Do I want to act from the attitude of that decision in the future?"
3. "Am I willing to let go of the decision now, and create a new reality?"
4. "Can I replace the decision with genuine good will toward that person?"
5. "What thought would I like to have instead?" Be specific.
6. Thank yourself for making the effort to change your mind.

Compassion and Forgiveness

One of the most important teachings of the Buddha is to develop compassion for yourself and others. My pal Margot tells me, "Carol, we're all bozos on this bus."

I love that image! I envision busloads of people all over the world, wearing big red clown noses, just for the fun of it, bouncing up and down in big old red school buses … holding on for dear life, just doing the best they can, and knowing "we're all on this Earth bus together. Let's help each other and make it wonderful."

For thirty years I commuted in lots and lots of California traffic. I love to drive, and on certain days I'd look over at other drivers and think, "Hi my friend, we're both going off to work together this morning. We're both doing our share to take care of our kids and families and each other." I'd just send them a lot of love.

I think that's one form of compassion—recognizing when something isn't really easy, but acknowledging the effort, love, and courage it takes to do what you believe is right.

It also has to do with knowing we're all in the same soup, with similar programming and misunderstandings of what's important. We've all been there at some time in our lives. The saints demonstrate that kind of compassion for each of us, and would like us to be gentle with each other in the same way.

When we're coming from compassion, we don't even need to forgive. We realize nothing is really out of order. Even all the imagined mistakes are necessary for learning our life lessons.

PART III

Practice the Presence of God

—Brother Lawrence

Chapter 10

The Beginning Saint Bridge

Living from Your God-Self

Once you've discovered YOU ARE GOD—living as you in your life—knowing and feeling this amazing Universal Truth—you realize the only thing left to do is to practice knowing you are inseparable from God.

A poet saint tells us, *"Be drunk on love!"*

Love yourself. Make new choices about what you think, what you do, and what you believe, until every moment of your life is totally saturated with the knowledge and light of your God-Self. Feel your God-Self now. Feel THAT! … THAT is You … YOU are That.

Always remember who you are. You've learned how your mind works. You've learned how to see God in yourself and others, and you've already learned some thinking practices and rituals that will help you maintain the awareness of your divinity.

Now it's time to practice what you know.

The Beginning Saint Mantra

"God is everywhere, in everything and everyone, including me."

This mantra is supercharged with the knowledge offered by the enlightened saints of all traditions.

You've heard "God is everywhere" (God is omnipresent, etc.) since you were a child, but growing up you didn't know how important it is, or its true meaning.

Now you know! It is yours forever and you can use it whenever you choose to remind yourself of your exquisite God-Self.

The first time I heard *"God is everywhere"* was in a Sunday school class in a little, white, steepled church in Inglewood, California. I was three years old.

My husband says he remembers hearing it for the first time when he was five—in a synagogue in Milwaukee, Wisconsin.

When was the first time you heard *"God is everywhere?"*

The mantra does not change. Its truth does not change. The difference is our understanding—our consciousness and conviction. The mantra is not a secret, but learning how to apply it is both the greatest gift and the biggest challenge.

In Chapter 7 you were introduced to the purpose and practice of repeating a sacred mantra.

True saints throughout history gave their students a phrase—a statement of truth, saturated with the divine energy of the saint—to help their students stay in the awareness of their God-Self.

The saints taught: *The understanding of the mantra, the goal of the mantra, and our God-Self—all are One.* There is no difference between the sacred knowledge embodied in the mantra *God is everywhere*, the person who repeats the mantra, and God.

The mantra confirms for us again that *there is no place where God is not.*

The person saying or singing the mantra experiences himself or herself as united—at One—with its essence and the wisdom and powers contained within it. His or her life begins to vibrate with the energy of the truth of the mantra.

When you repeat GOD IS EVERYWHERE to yourself, I AM GOD, I AM THAT, GOD LIVES WITHIN ME AS ME, AND WITHIN YOU AS YOU, you are recognizing inside yourself that God is indeed everywhere. Literally, GOD IS EVERYWHERE. With the power of your awakened knowledge you can transcend small-self beliefs and limitations of all kinds.

Take the jewel of the mantra out of your pocket. Use it and polish it every day. Let the power of the mantra shine through and guide you.

As you use it, notice how it changes what you believe about yourself. See limiting ideas drop away. Notice how recognizing that *God is everywhere* brings about changes in how you see your family, your friends, your adversaries, your boss, your co-workers—how you see the entire rest of the world.

The Beginning Saint Bridge

"The Beginning Saint Bridge," (The Bridge,) **"Knowing God is everywhere, in everything and everyone, including me"** is a short cut to your God-Self. It's the first step in a simple, four-step realization process for totally transforming your world. It is the connection between your usual awareness and the twenty-four-hour-a-day consciousness of your God-Self.

At any point in time when you notice a thought, sensation, or situation that doesn't feel right to you—one devoid of love or kindness—you can change it altogether by shifting your own awareness and what you choose to focus on. At last there's a way to break free from the chain of thoughts that keep you trapped.

My friend Susan asked me, "Isn't trying to change your thoughts a bit like moving the deck chairs on the Titanic—my ugly thoughts are still there in the background?"

"No, Susan," I replied, "It's not like that. You are all-powerful, and at any time you can choose to think ANY thought. All thoughts, good or bad, positive or negative, *loving or hateful,* are available for each of us to think. It's up to you which ones you choose."

Through practice we strengthen our ability to choose the thoughts we want to think. We can also choose to be free of thinking altogether, to let the mind rest in its essence.

A beginning saint soon learns he can spend decades trying to unravel a lifetime of family and societal programming, or he can take the shortcut to happiness by living in the consciousness of a saint now.

Great beings teach that you have more control over your destiny than you think. It's only you who puts a lid on your dreams.

A beginning saint learns to identify within her own mind the beliefs and behaviors that are out of alignment with her highest understanding. She uses The Bridge to quickly take her beyond these beliefs to a new awareness of her God-Self.

You can use The Bridge to actually move you from your limiting feelings and ideas about yourself to the state of your all-knowing God-Self—the unlimited, free saint within you.

How The Beginning Saint Bridge Works

Imagine for a moment that you are thinking a limiting thought such as, "I'm feeling overwhelmed by all the things I have to do today."

As soon as you think the thought, notice what feelings it creates in your mind and in your body. Do you notice a subtle, uncomfortable feeling? (When we are new at this we may not be aware that our thoughts actually create feelings in our bodies.)

As you notice it, you will start to feel a very clear distinction between a feeling generated by uplifting thoughts and one generated by limiting thoughts.

When you become aware that you don't like the feeling of "being overwhelmed" and that you want to change that feeling, you can use The Bridge in the following way:

The Four Steps of The Bridge

State to yourself:

Step One: Knowing God is everywhere, in everything and everyone, including me,

Step one asks you to contemplate what you feel when you realize God exists in all space, in all things, in everyone, including in your own mind and body.

Step Two: I let go of all thoughts, feelings, beliefs and judgments unlike my highest God-Self.

In this step you are releasing all the being-overwhelmed thoughts and feelings that perhaps have been manifesting as shortness of breath, sighing a lot, or tension in your shoulders.

You may find you have uncovered some old ideas—never having enough time, being stressed, being the target of a parent's or boss's anger. The thoughts may be unconscious—out of your awareness—or you may be experiencing them as images, memories, recollections of physical sensations and/or beliefs surfacing in your mind that are still shaping your experiences of life.

In previous chapters we have identified the many different kinds of thoughts, intentions, assumptions, judgments and decisions about ourselves and others that we think every day.

In this second step of The Bridge, we differentiate between the thoughts that feel peaceful and those we recognize as obstacles to the attainment of our highest God-Self state.

Such obstacles may include a decision or judgment we've made about someone or something—thought energy that has become so solidified as to become a part of our thinking process.

Mentally letting go of such "stuck" energy allows it to flow naturally, releasing us from any inflexibility or heaviness of thought.

Step Three: Knowing that all powers and characteristics of God live within me as me, I choose to (think, feel, have, do, or be) peaceful and capable of handling everything on my do list today.

You are reminded that all God's characteristics and powers are yours. You are a divine creator—there is no separation between you and God, and all unlimited potential creations existing in the universe—you have the power to summon and magnetize what you desire to yourself.

As you choose a new thought and say it to yourself, notice the corresponding feelings it creates in your body. Notice the transformation of the atmosphere around you. What you've done is identify the limiting thought and replace it with one that is more accurate and aligned with your God-Self than was the old thought.

Your new thought creates in subtle form the actual experience that you want to manifest.

Other possible choices you might have made in **Step Three**:

- to effortlessly have a day full of enjoyable people and experiences
- to feel powerful and in control of every interaction today
- to let go of having to be in control of everything and to be easy on myself
- to have an incredibly happy, peaceful, and productive day
- to feel calm and confident in all my tasks today

Become aware of the subtle shifts of feelings your new words have generated in your body. Use The Bridge to construct your day. Use it to transform self-imposed limitations. Use it to be even more powerful

Be creative. State what YOU really choose to think, feel, have, do and be in your life. You may decide to rest in an exquisite awareness of simply being, or you may choose to be wildly creative with your goals.

There are no limits to the ways in which you can use The Bridge. You have the power within your grasp.

Step Four: Thank you, God-Self for this shift in consciousness.

It's great to acknowledge your highest Self for responsibly transforming your life in the form of your thoughts now.

The Beginning Saint Bridge, the Cabbie, and Me

It was 2001, and I was just learning to apply the understanding that *God is everywhere.* It was Christmastime, ten months after 9/11, when I flew to London with Kathy, my childhood friend. We had a weekend-plus of shopping at Harrods and walking the sparkling streets of festive London, Christmas carols in the air. A glorious, if brief, adventure!

On departure day we dragged our baggage out to the curb of the hotel and called a taxi to take us to the train station, where we'd hop the train back to Heathrow.

The taxi arrived. I mumbled to Kathy, "Why isn't the taxi driver getting out of the cab to help us with our baggage?"

I'd immediately assumed the worst: "It must be because we're now over fifty, Kathy. No one will ever treat us like beautiful young women again. It's All Over!" (Of course I never spoke to the cabbie directly or found out if either my expectation or assumption was accurate.)

I grumpily opened the cab door myself, threw our bags into the back seat, and climbed in on top of them, still angry and sputtering. Kathy, my charming, never-critical friend, continued voicing her last-minute ideas about where we could travel to next.

I was having trouble shifting my mental gears. All the while she was talking I was still focused on the "terrible, inconsiderate English cabbie."

We finally arrived at Piccadilly Train Station. I fully expected that this time the cabbie would get out of the car, open the doors for us, and help us unload our baggage.

He didn't move! That confirmed my belief.

Kathy paid him, and I silently but furiously dragged the bags out of the cab and onto the curb.

The cabbie drove off while we clumsily gathered and pushed the odd assortment of luggage and packages into the station. Trains screeched and bells clanged as we stopped, stood still, caught our breath, and counted the two small suitcases and shopping bags, "One, two, three, four … OH, MY GOD! I left my purse in the cab!"

Panicked, I turned and ran hysterically to the taxi queue outside the station. Cabbies always get into line after they drop someone off. But not this time! Our cabbie was nowhere in sight!

I ran into the station to get the police. They said, "Sorry, lady, there are over three hundred different cab companies. They don't have cell phones. It's probably gone."

"You say you had EVERYTHING in your purse—your passport, $400 in cash, all your credit cards, and several hundred dollars in checks from your business? You had no time to deposit them before you left for the airport? Well, you know, identity theft is a big thing; you'll probably have your identity stolen, too, even your social security number!"

"Yes," I uttered helplessly, and, "Oh, horrors," I thought, "I don't even have my lipstick!"

In the meantime, my pal Kathy was worried she would miss her flight home to Chicago. With a kiss and a prayer she threw me some cash, enough for a train ticket to the airport. "I can't leave you here with nothing. I feel so bad," she cried, as we hugged and waved goodbye. Then she was gone, sprinting toward the train.

I asked the policeman if he would help me purchase the right ticket for Heathrow Airport. He was kind and very compassionate, but couldn't do more than that. "I'll take your phone number—you never know," he said.

I boarded the train and immediately went to work on myself. At first, all I could remember was the teaching, *"Your thoughts create your experience."*

I knew that if I wanted to feel better I should try to change my mind. I asked myself, "How do I change my mind … and in what way?"

I knew enough to recognize that my own miserable state of mind—my judgments and decisions—had created this unhappy fiasco. I thought, "I'll give The Bridge a chance," and started a conversation with myself:

"Carol, after all, no matter what happens, this is a perfect opportunity to see if changing your mind will actually create a different consequence, possibly a different feeling or energy in your life. And, besides, what do you have to lose?"

I continued, *"Carol, what actually did happen? You left your purse in the cab because you were too busy criticizing the cab driver and not paying attention to what you were doing. Was it the cab driver's fault? No, it was your fault. What are you going to do about it?"*

I had to think for a moment. *"Do you want to feel miserable and upset for the next couple of days, or do you have the willingness and motivation to change your thinking?"*

"I'm going to try to change my thinking, right now," I answered back to myself. "At least I can work on my own attitude—it couldn't get any worse."

"Instead of thinking bad things about yourself and bad things about the cabbie, Carol, see if you can change your feelings by changing your mind. Make a new choice about what you want to think and feel."

I desperately wanted to feel better. With much awkwardness and effort, I struggled to clearly and truthfully change my thinking about the event.

Beginning Saint Bridge to the Rescue!

I reminded myself of **Step One** of The Bridge: ***Knowing God is everywhere, in everything and everyone, including in me …***

that God, the all-pervasive, all-knowing, all-powerful energy, exists in the cabbie, in me, and in everyone and everything having to do with the situation.

Next, I contemplated **Step Two**. I struggled a bit with this one because I had to focus my mind. In the past I had allowed myself to think any wild thought any time. I had believed I was free and creative, but now realized I had some unruly thinking habits.

So, firmly taking charge of myself, I proceeded to **Step Two**: ***I let go of all thoughts, feelings, beliefs and judgments unlike my highest God-Self***. (I let go of all anger, decisions, and beliefs I'd had about the cabbie.) I chose to let go of defining the event as a "catastrophe" and view it as an *opportunity* to put The Bridge to work.

Taking that perspective allowed me to see I had jumped to conclusions about the cabbie instead of stepping into his shoes.

I asked myself, *"If you were to think thoughts more aligned with the qualities and characteristics of your God-Self, what would they be? What would you choose to think?"*

I began **Step Three**: Knowing that all characteristics and powers of God exist within me as me, ***I choose to*** *think grateful thoughts about the cabbie, like, 'He drove us peacefully and safely to the train station.'"* I wanted to have compassion for him and his job. *"I choose to give him the benefit of the doubt, be patient, understanding, generous and loving." (Maybe he doesn't feel good today … maybe handling baggage is not part of an English cabbie's job description.)*

I thought, *"When I get his address, I'll send him a lovely Indian scarf to keep him warm. I want to use this 'loss of my purse and all my identity' as an opportunity to see both the cabbie and me as equally divine, good people."*

When I did this, I felt surprisingly happy and free, totally aligned with my God-Self. Thanking my God-Self for this process seemed completely natural to me. I didn't even have to consciously remember **Step Four**—I felt so grateful for the change in my mind and the release of tension in my body.

I found myself easily thinking to myself, "**Step Four**—***Thank you, God-Self, for this shift in consciousness.***"

I relaxed into the train seat headed for Heathrow and sighed. I had no idea what to expect next, but noticed that all the anxiety, anger, and fear had dissolved. Using The Bridge had completely changed my own mental state, had melted the tension in my body, and had brought me into the present moment—home to my God-Self.

Minutes later, I found myself inexplicably able to get inside Heathrow Airport without my passport or any identification whatsoever. I boarded the plane—after 9/11—without a ticket, had great conversations with young men in the galley (naked of lipstick), got through U.S. Customs without a single piece of ID, and was able to get my car out of Long-Term Parking at the San Francisco Airport without my car keys, money, or a California driver's license.

To this day I can't remember how I got my car started, but I do know there was no toll to pay driving north across the Golden Gate Bridge.

Tuesday morning, an hour after I arrived at my office, I received a call on my answering machine from United Airlines in England. "We have your purse and your wallet and are sending it to you in three days."

Thursday morning a courier arrived with my purse. All of the cash, credit cards, IDs and checks were inside—even my lipstick.

I tried hard, but was never able get the address of the cabbie to thank him. I sent "A Cabbie Thank You Letter" to the Editorial Department of The London Times, but I don't think they ever printed it. I decided to just send the cabbie happy grateful wishes every once in a while—like right now.

I realize this story does not tell a life-shattering trauma, a story of death, grief, disease, starvation, physical abuse or addiction. It's the story of a seemingly superficial incident involving two "entitled" American women on an extravagant vacation, but ... it did happen exactly that way.

At the time, this experience with the cabbie and my own mind was the lesson life presented to me. It would be the lesson of my lifetime. Having already encountered cancer and a brain tumor, I knew that from then on out I would not create any more painful life events in order to confirm what I know is true.

My intention is for you to understand how the process works and to be able to apply it in your own life. My wish is for you to recognize the power that is already within you. Millions of people are demonstrating understanding of the process I call "The Bridge" and are making it work in their lives.

The "Beginning Saint Journal" to follow will give you lots of opportunity to apply this process directly to your own life.

You Create Your World

Getting Clear About What You Choose

Each of us has the freedom and ability to choose our own view of life, but most of us aren't really aware of all the myriad memories and visual images, let alone beliefs, judgments, decisions and other influences affecting our choices.

As a child, I'd often take a different point of view from my parents. I was one of those stubborn kids who had to do things *"my way,"* who had to *"find out for myself, Mom,"* before I'd believe anything she had to teach me. Most teenagers find themselves doubting and resisting their parent's views until they develop or discover their own. With me, it took years.

In the field of psychology this process is called *individuation*—a time in life when you need to find out for yourself what life is about and to establish self-confidence and certainty. It's a time of experimenting and exploring, searching and sorting.

When you recognize the thoughts and images that are no longer beneficial for you, you choose more uplifting thoughts and consciously let go of those that no longer bring you peace of mind or happiness. You eventually discover *you* are the one who is in charge of your mind.

The greatest saints dedicated huge portions of their lives to this process.

The individuation process is a great time to learn that the God-Self is actually God living perfectly as you: Practice stretching your beliefs about what is possible for you. Discover how truly rich and able you already are. Explore all the facets of yourself and your life.

For some people, individuation doesn't even begin until they are senior citizens ... sometimes it never happens. You may know someone like that yourself!

Putting It All Together

Using The Bridge to Shape the Life You Want

Exercise 28

Practice thinking through the four steps of The Bridge, and repeat them out loud to yourself.

Step One: Repeat to yourself, "**Knowing God is everywhere, in everything and everyone, including me,**

Step Two: I let go of all thoughts, feelings, beliefs and judgments unlike my highest God-Self.

Step Three: Knowing that all powers and characteristics of God live within me as me, I choose to (think, feel, have, do, or be) ______________

____

____

____

Step Four: Thank you, God-Self, for this shift in consciousness."

The "Beginning Saint Journal" in Chapter 11 gives you specific issues and situations in which to practice The Bridge in every facet of your life.

As you complete each practice session, notice what you are feeling, both before and afterwards. This will help you get clear about what you really believe, and will help you shape your thoughts and creations even more accurately.

If you are not wholeheartedly committed to what you say you want, you will know it by your feelings. That's okay, too. Awareness is the first step to transformation.

If you find yourself unable to let go of a disturbing visual image or a limiting thought, do not berate yourself. It's important to move at a pace that's real for you.

When you practice knowing and saying to yourself, *"God is everywhere, in everything and everyone, including me,"* you will start to recognize that *"everywhere"* means *"Everywhere"*—that God's energy, creativity, power and unlimited possibilities pervade all space and time, and are within you and available to you, and to everyone else, too.

You have the ability to create whatever you can imagine, and to mentally claim it for yourself. As you practice and expand your ability to imagine, your natural, innate powers will become increasingly self-evident.

The saints know that you have the ability to create *to the level of your understanding*, and as your understanding and willingness to receive expands, your ability to use your creativity, intellect, and powers will expand, too.

Remember that the only two obstacles to happiness are: 1) the belief that you are separate from God, and 2) the choices you make.

I can't emphasize enough, that when you take the time to constructively transform an idea about yourself, another, a situation or a condition, you will experience an automatic mind-shift, which in turn will create an equivalent change of feeling in your body.

It's a bit like getting a front-end alignment and wheel balancing. Aligned, balanced wheels allow your steering to be true and your ride smooth. Aligning your mind with your God-Self creates a stable mind. It allows the cells of your body to align with your innately perfect health.

Again, notice what you feel prior to using The Bridge and what feelings you experience afterwards. When you complete each issue in your Beginning Saint Journal you may want to record your insights in the section on Learning.

Practice the Bridge

As you master the four steps of The Bridge, your thoughts and ideas will synchronize with your true essence.

You'll get so good at it, you'll start catching yourself as soon as you feel the impulse of a painful, doubting, or limiting thought as soon as it flashes across your mind. You'll quickly remedy dual intentions, counter-intentions, and competing intentions so they no longer sabotage your dreams. You'll be able to release unwanted images, thoughts and feelings that seem to arise for no reason.

The mantra, *Knowing God is everywhere, in everything and everyone, including me,* points you to your own inner light. It embodies the most empowering knowledge—the basis for all creation.

Use the mantra to set the stage for your most creative God-Self to emerge. You'll easily locate any niggling, inaccurate beliefs in your life design, any upsetting memory, any incorrect decision, any disturbing feeling, any unconscious judgment of yourself or another, any belief in limitation of any kind, any obstacle, any delay and any counter-intention lurking in the back of your mind.

By ejecting and releasing such obstacles, you will refine and purify your consciousness. You will magnetize the energy of light and love to you.

The purpose of repeating **Step One** of The Bridge, "**God is everywhere, in everything and everyone, including me**," is to establish yourself in your essence.

Step Two, "**I let go of all thoughts, feelings, beliefs and judgments unlike my highest God-Self**,"allows you to clear the slate of old, extraneous patterns cluttering your mind.

Step Three, "**Knowing that all powers and characteristics of God live within me as me, I choose to (think, feel, have, do, or be) ...**," helps you choose what you *do* want.

State or write what you do want *in present time*. For instance, "*I have a great new job,*" rather than, "*I will have a great new job.*" Writing your desire in the present tense comes from the understanding that all you could want *already exists* in subtle form in the universe.

When you write your choice in present-tense form, you are simply claiming your desire as your own *now.*

Your choices create both your present life and your future.

Step Four, "Thank you, God-Self, for this shift in consciousness," creates a feeling of gratefulness and completes the healing process.

How Will My New Thoughts Show Up?

While you are thinking and constructing in your mind what you now know is available to you, visualize yourself actually experiencing it.

If you've been angry with another and want to change your reaction to them, visualize yourself and that person smiling or laughing together. Imagine seeing the person and allowing him or her to be there in your mind, free of upset.

What you are choosing already exists in subtle form, and the moment you think it, it will start to show up. You will see what you envision actually occur in your life. You are that powerful.

If what you desire is a happy feeling, you will start to experience it right away. If what you want is a three-dimensional object or an event to occur, it will manifest in accord with the extent of your trust in the process.

Begin by visualizing every aspect of what you desire—what it looks like, how it feels.

As in the pizza exercise we introduced earlier, it's important to describe your ideas in detail. Your God-Self recognizes the essence of your order and delivers it to you in the most beneficial form for you.

Since you are the designer and creator of your life, pay attention to how you are allowing or not allowing a desire to unfold. Have you placed a contingency thought in the way of it manifesting? Is it in competition with another desire?

What you want initially will show up as a perceptual change in your awareness. You'll notice both an emotional and a physical shift in feeling. You'll feel a warm glow and, as though you'd just been washed clean, a peaceful clarity.

If tears come, notice they are tears of recognition and the release of self-limiting feelings and thoughts. These may be the first results you experience.

Next, you may begin to enjoy what you want in a more tangible form. For instance, as you create a more open, accepting attitude, the same will automatically reflect back to you. The more you practice being conscious of what you are creating, the more you will notice it taking shape in your life.

In the stories below, you'll learn how others have used The Bridge to transform their thoughts and actualize their desires.

Diana, I'm Not a Puppet on a String

Diana found herself upset after watching a TV commercial advertising diabetes medication. She noticed that TV drug commercials made her doubt her own health. Not wanting to feel manipulated by the commercial she immediately used The Bridge.

She said to herself, (**Step One**) "**Knowing God is everywhere, in everyone and everything, including me**," (**Step Two**) "**I now let go of all thoughts, feelings, beliefs and judgments unlike my highest God-Self.**" (**Step Three**) "**Knowing that all powers and characteristics of God live within me as me, I choose** *health, knowing absolutely that my* *body is healthy at all times.* (**Step Four**) "**Thank you, God-Self, for this shift in consciousness.**"

Diana's results: "I decided that I did not want to fill my mind with TV commercials, murder mysteries, or disturbing movies. I realized I'm in charge of what I allow into my mind. Now I avoid watching or listening to negative fantasies, either from the media or my friends, and I consciously pay attention to what I'm thinking about during the day. I'm feeling so much more peaceful and powerful."

Gina's Challenge

Gina's frequent criticism of Sam was keeping her from having good feelings toward him. She noticed what she was doing and decided to change her behavior. In this example she chooses what she wants instead.

Gina said to herself, (**Step One**) "**Knowing God is everywhere, in everyone and everything, including me**," (**Step Two**) "**I now let go of all thoughts, feelings, beliefs and judgments unlike my highest God-Self.**" (**Step Three**) "**Knowing that all powers and characteristics of God live within me as me, I choose** *to freely communicate my needs to Sam and know he is completely capable of hearing my desires. I see him as a loving partner. He easily negotiates differences with me. I feel supported, comfortable, and content in his presence. I am choosing a happy and joyful relationship with Sam.* (You'll find that when you identify each of the ways you want to feel with a person, you are more likely to get what you want.) (**Step Four**) "**Thank you, God-Self, for this shift in consciousness.**"

Gina's results: "As I began seeing God within Sam, I noticed Sam becoming a better listener, more affectionate, more supportive, and more able to co-create with me."

At this time Gina feels more comfortable and happy with Sam. Did Sam change, or was there a change in Gina's attitude? Could it be that her transformed way of seeing Sam made room for him to actually be his best Self?

More Powerful Than She Thinks

Beginning Saint Susan is a bright energetic woman who comes from a family of high achievers. She told me, "I was able to identify my perfect job, and to materialize it right on the spot. I was hired immediately during my first interview at the firm."

Susan's new employer had recognized her abilities right away, but Susan, once on the job, began to let a hidden belief sabotage her: "I don't know enough to do the job. They'll just end up firing me."

So, with this counter-intention, Susan drove to work each day feeling nauseated, depressed, and anxious. At work, she compensated for her conviction that she "did not know enough" by overworking, which led to burn-out. Her belief was driving her discontent.

When Susan became able to see how her belief was actually limiting her enjoyment of her job, she replaced that thought with a new one.

Susan said to herself, (**Step One**) "**Knowing God is everywhere, in everyone and everything, including me**," (**Step Two**) "**I now let go of all thoughts, feelings, beliefs and judgments unlike my highest God-Self.**" (**Step Three**) "**Knowing that all powers and characteristics of God live within me as me, I choose** *to love my job, to learn my job rapidly, to know I am bright and capable, and to know I can do my job well and with ease. I choose to know my boss completely appreciates me,* *and that I am well compensated."* (**Step Four**) "**Thank you, God-Self, for this shift in consciousness.**"

Susan's results: Using The Bridge, Susan was totally restored to her innate confidence. She confided, "I realized that prior to using The Bridge I had planted a doubting seed in my own mind. I was the only one concerned about my performance. After using The Bridge I gave up being anxious, and re-focused all of my energy on the work instead. Now I'm doing a great job and they show me appreciation every day. I am not afraid of ever being fired, and I feel happy and content.

Johnny's Fear

Johnny, a man in his early forties, had learned to avoid jobs, women, or any situation that would require him to tell the truth. He was afraid of rejection, had little self-esteem, and had very few friends. His bosses couldn't trust him to set limits with customers, and women couldn't trust him to tell them what he wanted. When Johnny realized what he had been doing, he performed The Bridge.

He said to himself: (**Step One**) "**Knowing God is everywhere, in everyone and everything, including me,**" (**Step Two**) "**I now let go of all thoughts, feelings, beliefs and judgments unlike my highest God-Self.**" (**Step Three**) "**Knowing that all powers and characteristics of God live within me as me, I choose** *to have the courage to say what is true for me and also to accept or reject the suggestions of others. I choose to feel calm and peaceful. I'm confident that I have something of value to contribute to others."* (**Step Four**) "**Thank you, God-Self, for this shift in consciousness.**"

Johnny's results: "When I used The Bridge, the sick feelings in my stomach immediately dissolved. The anxious, fearful feelings dissipated. I became more courageous and freer as a person. I now feel more and more comfortable asking for what I want."

Seeing God in My Sister

Greg told me, "My sister is using drugs and is constantly asking for me to help her financially. I love her, but she feels like a burden to me. I worry about her health, her ability to pay the rent, and her ability to hold down a job." When Greg got clear about what he wanted, this is what he created:

He said to himself: (**Step One**) "**Knowing God is everywhere, in everyone and everything, including me,**" (**Step Two**) "**I let go of all thoughts, feelings, beliefs and judgments unlike my highest God-Self.**" (**Step Three**) "**Knowing that all powers and characteristics of God live within me as me, I choose** *to think of my sister as strong, healthy, able and self-sufficient.*" (**Step Four**) "**Thank you, God-Self, for this shift in consciousness.**"

Greg's results: "I was able to see how co-dependent I had been with my sister, and how my own thinking and behavior had contributed to my seeing her as irresponsible and helpless. I stopped financially taking care of her and began having more fun myself. On her own, my sister joined a twelve-step program and is on the road to recovery. I needed to transform my own judgments of her and see her as capable."

Lisa's New Start

Lisa is a creative, energetic woman who had developed and patented a product that helps both professional painters and novices do their jobs more effectively. She did not understand how to market her products, so her business spiraled downward. To avoid the embarrassment of failing, Lisa started using alcohol. She found herself unable to repay her investors or sell the product. She felt overburdened with financial loss. As a result of seeing things from the point of view of The Bridge, Lisa decided:

She said to herself: (**Step One**) "**Knowing God is everywhere, in everyone and everything, including me**," (**Step Two**) "**I let go of all thoughts, feelings, beliefs and judgments unlike my highest God-Self.**" (**Step Three**) "**Knowing that all powers and characteristics of God live within me as me, I choose** *to be a totally responsible and creative woman. I have the intention, resolve, and discipline to handle all challenges having to do with my life and my business.*" (**Step Four**) "**Thank you, God-Self, for this shift in consciousness.**"

Lisa's results: "I chose to stop using alcohol and to accept the ongoing support of my AA group. I love the teachings of the saints, and I am not letting anything stop me from my dream."

The first and biggest task Lisa had was to forgive herself. The second was to take responsibility for cleaning up her financial challenges. The third was to make the decision either to close her business or tackle it with a clean slate.

She chose a new start date for her business.

Can I Use The Bridge for Others?

The best thing you can do for others and yourself is to see God in all of you. Use The Bridge to change how you see other people. Rewrite your own vision of yourself and your view of them as *able, whole, healthy and resourceful.*

Ask yourself, "How would I want them to see me?"

Remind yourself of the highest truth of each person—as whole, capable, resourceful and intelligent, embodying the same qualities of God that you have discovered within yourself.

The greatest gift we can offer others is to see God in them—to change our own perception of them. Changing our own mind is more important than trying to change another's.

Remember, the saints know who we are. See yourself and others from the viewpoint of the beginning saint you are.

Can I Change Someone Else's Behavior?

I love the old saying, "Necessity is the mother of invention." Often it is not until someone feels he or she has no other options that the person finally reaches for a new perspective.

Your own job is to have patience with others and to remind yourself that they are totally creative and inventive and have the capacity to solve their own problems. This doesn't mean to be withholding, angry or unkind. It means to recognize the God-Self in everyone.

Two of God's qualities are perfect order and perfect timing. Remember to respect the timing of another's God-Self, knowing that he is going through his own growing process. While helping someone else, you must continue to trust that she is a capable human being. You must also continue to take care of your own finances, health, and other obligations.

In this way, you are seeing the God-Self in both of you. Establishing respect for another's timing will keep you from feeling responsible for him or her and give that person emotional room to change.

This doesn't mean to be a doormat and allow others to walk all over you. Remember your own God-Self and respect your own needs and wants. Honor your own timing and let the other person know when something you want is important to you.

If another person is not making choices in the direction of his or her highest God-Self, even if you love the person, you always have the choice of whether or not to live or work with him or her.

Can I Use The Bridge for Different Issues?

There are no people, places, or things where God does not exist. There are no subjects, no feelings, or thoughts where The Bridge cannot be used.

The Bridge applies to any thought, any emotion, and any area of your life where your goal is to think, feel, create and take action from your God-Self.

Is Choosing All I Need to Do?

The truth is, "YES!"

However, some of us feel the need to erase the "old marks" on the blackboard before writing a new story.

But, as we practice transforming existing thoughts, feelings, beliefs and judgments into what we want to think instead, we find ourselves increasingly quick to notice "glitches" (untruths) and to shift our perspective without having to expend a lot of effort re-examining *every* negative thought or feeling we've ever had. We gain the awareness and skill to simply *move our consciousness* to its highest knowing.

Similarly, using an artist's eye, on shifting our perspective we may find ourselves incorporating existing lines and smudges into a totally new concept, seeing the old globs of paint as something rich and interesting—transformed.

It's all about shifting perspective, and all we have to do is *do it*.

The Bridge is an unlimited process for connecting with your God-Self and creating the life you desire. As your creative skills grow, your willingness to choose and accept the best will increase. You will recognize when your intentions are clear, and you will see that there are no limits to what you can have, do, or be in the world. Since your imagination is limitless, there will be no dimensions in which you cannot create.

Remember, the only one who places limits on your creations is you. Have fun!

Becoming a More Able Creator

Beginning saints contemplate and refine their choices. Here are some tips for maximizing your "Beginning Saint Bridge" creations:

1. Allow yourself to embellish your visualizations to include each aspect of having, doing, and being what you really want.

2. See yourself having it. What would it look like?
3. Imagine yourself doing and being it. How would you experience it?
4. Describe how you want the experience to feel.
5. Imagine how it would affect your day, your relationships, and your finances.
6. How great could you allow yourself to feel?
7. Imagine how this desire could positively affect your health, your family members, and friends.
8. Be aware of any little nuances of thought that are not accurate from the perspective of your God-Self. Be willing to drop them completely.
9. Be an even more powerful creator. As you practice visualizing, writing and creating what you do want, The Bridge will become easier and easier for you. Eventually you will see your ideas beautifully and richly unfolding.
10. Shape your desires by adding all the qualities you really want. At times, you also may want to simplify your life to fit new values and new awareness.
11. Use The Bridge until you feel a balanced, happy feeling inside. More and more you will be able to achieve a contented state of being.

If, after you have used The Bridge, you still feel a glitch or "funniness" in the pit of your stomach, realize there is probably a self-limiting thought or feeling still stuck there.

Practice being really clear and specific about what you desire. Then, when you choose, you will feel a sweet sensation of peace inside.

There's One More Thing …

Learning to Accept

How many of you have rejected a gift or relationship by believing you didn't deserve it, shouldn't have it, or felt guilty for having it? You may have minimized the part you played in earning it, or for some unknown reason just couldn't allow yourself to feel *that good*. Can you allow yourself to receive all the wonderful things the world wants to give to you?

Being able to accept good things goes hand in hand with choosing them, because it creates a continuous flow.

If accepting good things makes you uncomfortable, just practice being grateful and those awkward feelings will dissolve. It's essential that you honor yourself and see God in yourself just as you are.

The Bridge as your innate "biofeedback" mechanism allows you to be in touch with your innermost self. As you practice the knowing of a saint, you will learn to trust your God-Self more and more. You will be mastering your mind.

Using your own God powers via The Bridge, you will get unstuck from old feelings, beliefs, and thinking habits that no longer serve you. You will have a fresh start in every moment.

I'm Not Willing

One day I told my friend Jake, "Since you can only think one thought at a time, how about thinking the best about yourself—the truth about your God-Self?"

Jake made an obscene gesture to let me know he couldn't do that.

Laughing, but somewhat distressed, I said, "Why not? You know you have the ability to feel great about yourself and yet you don't seem to want to."

"That's right," he said. "I just want to get this life over with. It's too hard. I have to fight too hard to get what I want. No one listens to me."

Jake intellectually knew the truth about himself—that he is a divine being, but he chose to blame others and hold on to resentments rather than muster the courage to choose happiness. Since he had the ability to think any thought, he could choose to think small if he wished.

Jake refused to try **The** Bridge. He recognized that he wasn't willing to let go of old thoughts and beliefs in order to create something new.

It takes not only choice, but also courage and discipline, to be willing to let go of ingrained habits of whining and blaming to make way for something positive. We each have the power of choice.

My own spiritual challenge is to know that Jake is also a beginning saint, doing exactly what he needs to do in order to learn and grow.

Most of us have had moments of feeling stubborn and stuck. I know that Jake, too, is God in his form, and that he has the ability to choose. I can offer him compassion.

We've all been there. We may have felt the same way or have not been ready to experience our God-Self full-time.

We're always free to keep our limited ideas at the same time as knowing we are unlimited, divine beings. Since we are living this life as human beings, we know that both realities are true simultaneously: we may have limiting thoughts yet know we are divine.

We know that others may speak and act from their limited ideas of Self too, but we also know that they are divine. As we recognize, however, that our thoughts create consequences, we know the futility of remaining in negative states.

If, like Jake, you notice you simply are not willing to let go of old beliefs, then continue doing what you are doing! The co-founder of Alcoholics Anonymous, Bill Wilson, was known to say, *When you get sick and tired of being sick and tired, then maybe, just maybe, you'll try something new.*

Polishing the Facets of Your Life

Your life is composed of hundreds of amazing and radiant facets, like a diamond, all emanating from the same point of God. Each facet reflects an exquisite and creative aspect of your Divine nature. Some are bright and shiny and reflect light perfectly. Others may need a little scrubbing and polishing.

Try creating sweet, loving, and generous thoughts towards your own self. A saint sees human beings and all life forms from a compassionate viewpoint.

In your "Beginning Saint Journal" in Chapter 11 you will have an opportunity to shift what you think in many important areas of your life.

You'll have a chance to re-examine how you approach your relationships and work, and how you view yourself, your health and your body. You may find yourself creating "new beginnings" in many facets of your life such as friendships, groups, finances, and your environment.

You'll learn to use The Bridge with each facet, allowing yourself to spend some time contemplating and possibly reshaping many of them.

Be generous with yourself. I recommend that you polish your facets little by little, systematically purifying and aligning each one with your new beginning-saint perspective—your God-Self.

Your skill will increase the more you practice letting go of obstacles and identifying what you truly want.

Over time, changing a limiting thought to a clear new thought will become automatic for you. Notice how empowered you feel each time you complete working on a facet with The Bridge.

How Will I Recognize The Results of My Shift in Consciousness?

When you change the way you see something, you automatically experience a subtle, but sometimes dramatic, shift in your feelings. Amazingly, a small movement in consciousness can shift your health, your relationships, your whole body and even your whole life.

You will feel a lovely, calm, clear, and even exciting feeling inside when such a shift happens.

What's interesting is that shifts can be ongoing, with emotional and physical benefits unfolding over an entire lifetime. Recall a time you made a negative judgment about someone, but later became friends with that same person.

Notice similar shifts of feelings in your body both before and after you apply The Bridge. Acknowledge your Great Self with each shift.

As you use The Bridge for transforming your thoughts, great things may happen before your eyes. You will find yourself re-examining your view of major areas of your life.

I recommend you review the entire list of *Life Facets* before starting the process. Then you can select facets of special interest to you, or approach them all in sequence.

In addition to the facets listed, you may wish to create some of your own. Spend time contemplating each one. Notice what you feel as you respond to each step of The Bridge.

Remember, the saints know who you are. Saints see the perfection in you.

As a beginning saint you are learning how to see that same whole, perfect God-Self in everyone, and especially in you.

Coach the saint within you by making it an ongoing practice to review and rewrite your life facets every few weeks or months. This practice will help you stay on track with your goals.

If you feel resistant to a specific facet, such as, perhaps, seeing the greatness in another, give yourself a break and attempt The Bridge at a later time. Be easy on yourself.

Most of all, acknowledge the beginning saint in yourself and be sweet and respectful towards yourself.

Your timing is already perfect, even if you can't see it.

Many beginning saints use The Bridge to reformulate their overall lifestyle. Realizing they have the power to change how they view life, their inner enemies of anger, lust, greed, envy or fear simply fall away, to be replaced by new feelings of trust, confidence, forgiveness and love.

Remember that because you are God in the form of you, your highest God-Self is already pure. You are a beginning saint—powerful, unlimited, loving, compassionate, patient, generous, steadfast, intelligent and courageous! Take the time to enjoy your radiant self and have a great time!

Self-Effort
And
Grace…
Two
Wings
Of
A
Bird

Chapter 11

My Beginning Saint Journal

Practicing the Beginning Saint Bridge

As you polish and purify your life facet by facet, allow yourself to try on and savor the spectrum of thoughts and feelings that arise. Notice if they are sweet, pungent, sour, tart, hot, spicy or bitter—if they register as peaceful or charged.

As you read each facet (issue) in your journal, notice what feelings come up: If you feel calm and unhooked from a facet, simply be aware of your peaceful feeling and move on to the next facet.

If you feel even a little agitated as you read your journal, be aware that there is probably something about that subject that you might like to change.

Look at what comes up for you. What feelings or images arise?

You will experience the most benefit from using The Bridge when you approach each facet slowly and thoughtfully. Be aware if you are rushing or taking on too many at a sitting. The more deeply you contemplate a facet, the more beneficial the transformation can be for you. Start with one facet at a time and contemplate each facet at your own pace.

As you read each facet, ask yourself: Do I have some "charge" on this subject? Is this issue something I would like to change? Would I like to think and feel more at ease about this subject?"

If you answer "yes" to any of these questions, proceed to use The Bridge, noticing your physical and your emotional feelings before and after using it. What does your heart tell you?

Do you need more time to contemplate what comes up for you? Are you taking on too much, or can you proceed to another facet?

When you've completed the four steps, you may want to make a note of anything you've learned about yourself in the process—any insights or realizations you've had. State how you will implement this new understanding in your life.

Life Facets

1. My relationship with myself

Step One: Repeat to yourself, "Knowing God is everywhere, in everything and everyone, including me,

Step Two: I let go of all thoughts, feelings, beliefs and judgments unlike my highest God-Self.

Step Three: Knowing that all powers and characteristics of God live within me as me, I choose (to think, feel, have, do, or be) ________________

____

____

____

Step Four: Thank you, God-Self, for this shift in consciousness."

I learned: ____

____

2. My relationship with my body

Step One: Repeat to yourself, "Knowing God is everywhere, in everything and everyone, including me,

Step Two: I let go of all thoughts, feelings, beliefs and judgments unlike my highest God-Self.

Step Three: Knowing that all powers and characteristics of God live within me as me, I choose (to think, feel, have, do, or be) ________________

____

____

____

Step Four: Thank you, God-Self, for this shift in consciousness."

I learned: ____

____

3. My relationship with my mother

Step One: Repeat to yourself, "Knowing God is everywhere, in everything and everyone, including me,

Step Two: I let go of all thoughts, feelings, beliefs and judgments unlike my highest God-Self.

Step Three: Knowing that all powers and characteristics of God live within me as me, I choose (to think, feel, have, do, or be) ______________

____

____

____

Step Four: Thank you, God-Self, for this shift in consciousness."

I learned: ______________________________

____

4. My relationship with my father

Step One: Repeat to yourself, "Knowing God is everywhere, in everything and everyone, including me,

Step Two: I let go of all thoughts, feelings, beliefs and judgments unlike my highest God-Self.

Step Three: Knowing that all powers and characteristics of God live within me as me, I choose (to think, feel, have, do, or be) ______________

____

____

____

Step Four: Thank you, God-Self, for this shift in consciousness."

I learned: ______________________________

____

5. My relationship with my partner

Step One: Repeat to yourself, "Knowing God is everywhere, in everything and everyone, including me,

Step Two: I let go of all thoughts, feelings, beliefs and judgments unlike my highest God-Self.

Step Three: Knowing that all powers and characteristics of God live within me as me, I choose (to think, feel, have, do, or be) ______________

____

____

____

Step Four: Thank you, God-Self, for this shift in consciousness."

I learned: ______________________________

____

6. My relationship with my emotions

Step One: Repeat to yourself, "Knowing God is everywhere, in everything and everyone, including me,

Step Two: I let go of all thoughts, feelings, beliefs and judgments unlike my highest God-Self.

Step Three: Knowing that all powers and characteristics of God live within me as me, I choose (to think, feel, have, do, or be) ______________

____

____

____

Step Four: Thank you, God-Self, for this shift in consciousness."

I learned: ______________________________

____

7. My relationship with my work or school

Step One: Repeat to yourself, "Knowing God is everywhere, in everything and everyone, including me,

Step Two: I let go of all thoughts, feelings, beliefs and judgments unlike my highest God-Self.

Step Three: Knowing that all powers and characteristics of God live within me as me, I choose (to think, feel, have, do, or be) ____________

____

____

____

Step Four: Thank you, God-Self, for this shift in consciousness."

I learned: ______________________________

____

8. My relationship with my family member

Step One: Repeat to yourself, "Knowing God is everywhere, in everything and everyone, including me,

Step Two: I let go of all thoughts, feelings, beliefs and judgments unlike my highest God-Self.

Step Three: Knowing that all powers and characteristics of God live within me as me, I choose (to think, feel, have, do, or be) ____________

____

____

____

Step Four: Thank you, God-Self, for this shift in consciousness."

I learned: ______________________________

____

9. My relationship with my boss

Step One: Repeat to yourself, "Knowing God is everywhere, in everything and everyone, including me,

Step Two: I let go of all thoughts, feelings, beliefs and judgments unlike my highest God-Self.

Step Three: Knowing that all powers and characteristics of God live within me as me, I choose (to think, feel, have, do, or be) ______________

____

____

____

Step Four: Thank you, God-Self, for this shift in consciousness."

I learned: ______________________________

____

10. My relationship with my co-worker

Step One: Repeat to yourself, "Knowing God is everywhere, in everything and everyone, including me,

Step Two: I let go of all thoughts, feelings, beliefs and judgments unlike my highest God-Self.

Step Three: Knowing that all powers and characteristics of God live within me as me, I choose (to think, feel, have, do, or be) ______________

____

____

____

Step Four: Thank you, God-Self, for this shift in consciousness."

I learned: ______________________________

____

11. My relationship with my friend

Step One: Repeat to yourself, "Knowing God is everywhere, in everything and everyone, including me,

Step Two: I let go of all thoughts, feelings, beliefs and judgments unlike my highest God-Self.

Step Three: Knowing that all powers and characteristics of God live within me as me, I choose (to think, feel, have, do, or be) ____________

____

____

____

Step Four: Thank you, God-Self, for this shift in consciousness."

I learned: ____________

____

12. My relationship with my home

Step One: Repeat to yourself, "Knowing God is everywhere, in everything and everyone, including me,

Step Two: I let go of all thoughts, feelings, beliefs and judgments unlike my highest God-Self.

Step Three: Knowing that all powers and characteristics of God live within me as me, I choose (to think, feel, have, do, or be) ____________

____

____

____

Step Four: Thank you, God-Self, for this shift in consciousness."

I learned: ____________

____

13. My relationship with another person

Step One: Repeat to yourself, "Knowing God is everywhere, in everything and everyone, including me,

Step Two: I let go of all thoughts, feelings, beliefs and judgments unlike my highest God-Self.

Step Three: Knowing that all powers and characteristics of God live within me as me, I choose (to think, feel, have, do, or be) ______________

____

____

____

Step Four: Thank you, God-Self, for this shift in consciousness."

I learned: ______________________________

____

14. My relationship with my education or skill

Step One: Repeat to yourself, "Knowing God is everywhere, in everything and everyone, including me,

Step Two: I let go of all thoughts, feelings, beliefs and judgments unlike my highest God-Self.

Step Three: Knowing that all powers and characteristics of God live within me as me, I choose (to think, feel, have, do, or be) ______________

____

____

____

Step Four: Thank you, God-Self, for this shift in consciousness."

I learned: ______________________________

____

15. My relationship to a personal goal

Step One: Repeat to yourself, "Knowing God is everywhere, in everything and everyone, including me,

Step Two: "I let go of all thoughts, feelings, beliefs and judgments unlike my highest God-Self.

Step Three: "Knowing that all powers and characteristics of God live within me as me, I choose (to think, feel, have, do, or be) ______________

____

____

____

Step Four: "Thank you, God-Self, for this shift in consciousness."

I learned: ______________________________

____

16. My Relationship to ______________ that annoys me

Step One: Repeat to yourself, "Knowing God is everywhere, in everything and everyone, including me,

Step Two: "I let go of all thoughts, feelings, beliefs and judgments unlike my highest God-Self.

Step Three: "Knowing that all powers and characteristics of God live within me as me, I choose (to think, feel, have, do, or be) ______________

____

____

____

Step Four: "Thank you, God-Self, for this shift in consciousness."

I learned: ______________________________

____

Important Additional Relationships To Address Using The Beginning Saint Bridge

1. My relationship with my health
2. My relationship with my home
3. My relationship with my child
4. My relationship with another family member
5. My relationship with my career or job
6. My relationship with my employer or employee
7. My relationship with my community
8. My relationship with my neighbor(s)
9. My relationship with money or finances
10. My relationship to my roles in life
11. My relationship to my general environment
12. My relationship to a habit
13. My relationship to self-discipline
14. Having a romantic relationship
15. My relationship to animals
16. Giving compliments to others
17. Being a parent
18. Being a caregiver
19. Feeling included in a family, workgroup, etc.
20. My relationship to an organization or group

My Feelings

1. Trusting ______________
2. Having courage
3. Feeling happy
4. Experiencing criticism
5. Receiving praise

6. Feeling joy
7. Feeling excited or passionate
8. Feeling pain
9. Feeling loss
10. Feeling secure/safe
11. Feeling emotional support
12. Contentment with life
13. Feeling physical support
14. Feeling in balance
15. Feeling I have a choice
16. Self-acceptance
17. Self confidence
18. Feeling in control
19. Avoidance
20. Trusting in life
21. Trusting my body
22. Trusting my God-Self
23. Trusting my feeling heart
24. Feeling powerful
25. Affection
26. Intimacy/closeness
27. Sexuality
28. Gratitude
29. Feeling close to someone
30. Other people's habits
31. Sensitivity to noises, smells, etc.
32. Annoying behaviors
33. Feeling authentic
34. Feeling compassion
35. Forgiving another
36. My emotional health
37. Freedom to have, do or be what I choose
38. Trusting my intuition
39. Feeling loveable

40. Accepting changes in myself
41. Attitudes towards gender issues
42. Taking risks
43. Having opinions
44. Issues around birth
45. Feeling equal with others
46. Anxiety or fear

My Attitudes

1. Attitude towards a person
2. Attitude towards an issue
3. Attitude towards a challenge
4. Belief about death
5. Seeing something newly
6. Moving in a new direction
7. Commitment to ________________
8. Fun and recreation
9. Exercise
10. Longing for closeness
11. Letting go of the past
12. Looking forward to the future
13. Competition
14. Asking for help from others
15. Beliefs about men
16. Beliefs about women
17. Friendships
18. Attitude towards change
19. Attitude towards children
20. Attitude towards seniors
21. Prejudice attitude of any kind
22. Sexist thinking and/or behavior
23. Racist thinking and/or behavior

24. My beliefs about fat, skinny, short or tall, young or old
25. Philosophical conflicts
26. Religious differences
27. Beliefs about illness
28. Violence or abuse of any kind (thoughts or actions)
29. Staying healthy
30. Having enough energy
31. Keeping agreements and commitments
32. Having enough time
33. Attitude toward marriage
34. Attitude towards being single

My Abilities

1. Feeling competent
2. Freedom to communicate anything to anyone
3. Assertiveness
4. Ability to prioritize
5. My intelligence/intellect
6. Creativity
7. Educational skills
8. Accomplishments
9. Leadership ability
10. Public speaking
11. Honesty
12. Authenticity
13. Ability to negotiate
14. Conflict resolution
15. Problem-solving skills
16. Memory
17. Work performance

18. Likeability
19. Giving compliments
20. Ability to create everything I need and want
21. Ability to make others laugh
22. Wisdom
23. Ability to offer compassion
24. Ability to offer advice
25. Having abundance
26. Ability to comprehend
27. Ability to listen
28. Ability to give and receive love
29. Ability to empathize
30. Caring of self and/or others
31. Accomplishing my goals

Subjects to consider

1. My age
2. Having everything I need
3. My social life
4. A challenge ________________
5. My ability to focus on ________________
6. My appetite
7. Sexuality
8. Politics
9. Lifestyle
10. Gifts
11. Taxes
12. Travel
13. Hobbies
14. Finding life meaningful
15. Having a purpose

Additional Life Facets, Issues and Goals

There may be specific other facets in your life that you want to refine. Maybe there are certain feelings or automatic responses you'd like to change, such as the way you approach a subject, a person, or a painful or traumatic event.

You might want to do a clean sweep of every area of your life or transform a story or identity that no longer feels like who you are.

Feel free to create your own facets or subject areas. Some people might wish to include their most current upset, perhaps dealing with negativity, loneliness, or depression.

Others may want to focus on issues surrounding independence, abundance, transformation, pleasure, wisdom, love, success, new life, flow, circulation, guidance, partnership or teamwork.

The Bridge is yours now. It's in your bones. You can use it to create every dream you've had in the past as well as infinite new ones. The power has always been yours. Now it's there when you wish to use it.

In the final chapter of *Beginning Saint* you'll have a chance to contemplate a whole new world for yourself—possibly one you've never conceived of before—perhaps one in which your own highest God-Self plays the starring role.

.......when the mind is at peace and the heart leaps to the supreme truth, when all the disturbing thought-waves in the mind-stuff have subsided and there is unbroken flow of peace and the heart is filled with the bliss of the absolute, when thus the truth has been seen in the heart, then this very world becomes an abode of bliss.

—Swami Venkatesananda
The Concise Yoga Vasistha

Chapter 12

Returning to Camelot

I had just begun college when John F. Kennedy was President. It was the 1960s, and for many Americans it was an era bursting with enthusiasm, generosity, and hope.

During the few brief years of "Camelot," the nation experienced a glimpse of what is possible when consciousness wakes up. For the first time in history, millions of young people went to college. In an attempt to correct social injustices, civil rights activists courageously got out the vote. Americans even put a man on the moon.

President Kennedy's request, *"Ask not what your country can do for you; ask what you can do for your country,"* inspired thousands to apply to the Peace Corps. It was a completely exciting and inspiring time in my own life. The country believed in itself, and I was confident that helping others was what I wanted to do most with my life.

For me, personally, however, life, falling in love, and babies, postponed my "making a difference," at least the kind of difference I envisioned. Tempered by the immediate need to earn a living and take care of children, I did not get to be a "real" hippie, and the Peace Corps had to wait.

Then, within moments it seemed, my generation witnessed the deaths of John F. Kennedy, Martin Luther King, and Robert Kennedy, and the Vietnam War intruded on the dream.

"This doesn't make any sense!" we cried.

Despair pushed many of us to search for answers within. We knew great things were possible. We had put a man on the moon, and we believed that, "of course there are enough resources for everyone on Earth." We knew that answers lay in our willingness to do what's necessary to solve the problems of poverty and hunger, and to provide education and health care for everyone.

But many of us were still trapped by fear of change and old beliefs and thinking habits, and millions of others used similar justifications to keep them from their dreams.

I realized that in order to follow Gandhi's challenge, *"Be the change you wish to see in the world,"* I'd first have to learn how to change my own mind and myself. I'd have to let go of a library's worth of beliefs in limitation and concepts of scarcity, and remind myself that unlimited options and creativity dwell within each person, including in me, and that I could develop the skill to control my own unruly mind.

On a daily basis I struggled with questions like, "What kind of change would have to happen for people to live peacefully with one another? What kind of a difference could I personally make that would contribute to the end of wars and famines forever and that could empower all humanity with true power over adversity and give all people genuine self esteem and a healthy, sustainable lifestyle?"

These questions continued to prod me like a blister that wouldn't heal. Every time I contemplated them, the inner answer that came up was, *"Learn how to change your own mind, Carol; then help other people change their minds."*

Changing The World

Sherry Anderson and Paul Ray, co-authors of *The Cultural Creatives: How 50 Million People are Changing the World,* tell us that "Cultural Creatives" are conscious, aware people who confront the attitudes and behaviors that get in the way of having a happy life. They deal head on with such obstacles. They ask themselves, "What beliefs are stopping me from making the difference I want?" They ask each of us to consider what understandings will release our stuck positions and mobilize us. "What beliefs, decisions, and ideas constitute what's real for you?" They encourage us to change our stances and be willing to let go of outdated habits and thinking patterns.

Anderson and Ray write, "Changing a world view literally means changing what you think is real. This requires changes in values, fundamental life priorities, ways you spend time and money, and changes in livelihood. The real leaders of the next century will be those people who have done their *deep spiritual work* as well as their work in the world and are able to combine the two."

The authors' research shows how large segments of people all over the world, right now, are making constructive choices that are bringing about more peace, health, play, love, joy and abundance for everyone.

I believe that *"the deep spiritual work"* they speak of means developing the skills to change our thinking, becoming aware that we are IT, and practicing the *Presence of God* with each other on the planet.

Creating a New Worldview

In his book, *The Holographic Universe,* Michael Talbot relates a study by the psychologist Chet Snow: "Snow had interviewed 2,500 psychics about the kind of world they saw in the future. Four distinct themes emerged suggesting several potential futures, or holoverses, *'forming in the gathering mists of fate.'"*

Talbot writes, *"We create our own destiny, both individually and collectively. The scenarios are a glimpse into the various potential futures the human race is creating for itself en masse."* He says that we should spend time believing in and envisioning a positive future. *"If we are continually shaping our future physical reality by today's collective thoughts and actions, then the time to wake up to the alternative we have created is now. Which do we want for our grandchildren? Which do we want perhaps to return to ourselves someday?"*

A World Full of Saints

A Guiding Story to Uplift All Mankind

Joseph Campbell, the great twentieth century mythologist, taught, *"A society without a guiding story cannot function coherently. Civilizations fall apart when they do not have a cultural story to help them make sense of life."*

I searched recent literature and discussed this idea with my closest friends. Then one day I remembered the last time I'd heard Swami Muktananda speak in person. In a goodbye program at the end of the summer in 1982, he spoke about his wish for *a world full of saints.*

I remembered that a giant gong had reverberated in my heart when I heard him speak his vision. *"A world full of saints,"*

I thought, "Yes, that's it! That is the great guiding story, the purpose of our human life, isn't it?"

"But how do we move towards that goal?" I asked myself. "What would it look like? What would it feel like? How do we achieve such a world, such a state of being?"

Thinking about it twenty-five years later, I can see Muktananda's vision already unfolding perfectly. A metamorphosis is already happening in every corner of the world. People of all spiritual persuasions are discovering their true identity—their equality, power, intelligence and true inner freedom.

A world full of saints is unfolding. It's a world full of human beings grounded in the truth and living in that awareness twenty-four hours a day. *A world full of saints* consists of a world full of people who know they are God, and they know you are, too. All their actions come from the awareness that *God is everywhere.*

The true saints of all traditions have done their personal spiritual work, and through their teachings have given us the fruits of their wisdom and blessings. When they taught us that *God is everywhere,* they gave us "the jewel of great price," with the power to achieve *a world full of saints.* They gave us the knowledge of our God-Self. They taught us who we are, how our minds work, the value of self-discipline and of kindness and selfless service to others. They taught us how to live a divine life.

As beginning saints we are gradually awakening to the true understanding of "*God is everywhere.*" Our planet is peopled by loving and powerful beings who want the best for every living inhabitant on earth. Their hearts and minds are focused on loving and caring for God within everyone—in every country across the globe.

To bring about this guiding vision of *a world full of saints,* our job is to practice bridging the gap between our fearful small self and our God-Self, until we live from our highest God-Self all the time. We must cooperate with each other to create communities that share in the abundance of the earth and enrich and support the best in every global citizen.

The guiding story, *a world full of saints*—its vision and intention—is already unifying and shaping our destiny and our planet in beautiful and positive ways. It gives new meaning and purpose to all life, and is inspiring millions of practical humanitarian projects that uplift everyone everywhere.

One lovely example of people making the vision real arrived recently in the mail. In a funding request for UNICEF, the author of the letter said, "I'm not writing you today to focus on the painful realities. Instead I'd like to show you how your support has the potential to change the facts. UNICEF buys tents, blankets, pots, and provides high-energy biscuits and powdered milk to hungry children … purifies water and digs new water wells … stocks schoolbooks … purchases and distributes vaccines … and talks to kids about HIV/AIDS prevention. Blanket by blanket, book by book, water well by water well, UNICEF takes very ordinary items to places where they become extraordinary … and these simple tasks transform the world. Thank you for your ongoing commitment to the world's children."

A request like that inspires us and reminds us that the world's children are our own. Thought by thought, one person at a time, the whole planet is becoming *a world full of saints.*

Preparing For a World Full of Saints

What belief and emotional shifts do you need to make in order to manifest the state of a saint in your own life, in your relationships, in your work? What will you do to live 24 hours a day in the consciousness of your highest Self?

Can you believe in the possibility that *everyone* can win?

We see an evolution of our country's governing system also unfolding as our consciousness grows and expands.

Notice how your beliefs about the world have changed since you began to see yourself and others from the knowingness of a saint. Are you ready to let go of the past? Are you choosing to think new thoughts?

As you practice transforming outdated cultural beliefs, the purity of your God-Self will emerge even more brightly.

What lifestyle and values match your new world vision? What old decisions are you willing to change?

Notice how you feel when you make shifts in your lifestyle and values.

What nurturing and rituals are you adding to your life that will help you to experience your God-Self more often?

Coming Full Circle

In *Beginning Saint* we have studied the teachings of the saints and sages of many traditions and discovered their common, unifying principles, especially that *God is everywhere and exists perfectly in each of us.* These evolved beings have pointed the way to a glorious future—*a world full of saints*—where everyone knows that he or she *is The Divine Presence* itself.

In *Beginning Saint* you've learned you are God—that we all are God living as individual creations in unlimited and exquisite forms, evolving from lifetime to lifetime in never-ending, infinitely expanding universes of love.

Now we have arrived at a point in our evolution where, knowing we are inseparable from God, we can consciously shape both our individual and global destinies. We know what we need to do to manifest *a world full of saints* for ourselves.

When it's time to move on from this planet we will no longer be afraid of dying, but will joyfully anticipate the coming adventure, fully trusting that we are eternal, immortal God-beings who cannot die.

I'm so grateful to have been born in this century, to have had the mother-teacher I did, to be able to pursue my highest dreams, and to have learned from fully realized saints who have given me everything for all lifetimes.

I hope that I have ignited in you the longing to know your own greatness.

My wish for you is mastery over your own life and the ecstasy of knowing and experiencing your own radiant God-Self.

Bibliography

Abbott, Justin. *The Life of Tukaram Motilal.* New Delhi: Banarsidass Publishers,1930.

Barks, Coleman. *A Year With Rumi.* San Francisco, California: Harper Collins Publishers, 2006: 55.

Bartlett, Richard. *The Physics of Miracles. Hillsboro, Oregon: Beyond Words,2009*

Benson, Herbert. *The Relaxation Response.* New York: William Morrow and Co., 1978.

China Healthways Newsletter, China Healthways Institute, Spring 2000, Number 101: 1.

Crowell, Thomas Y. *Emerson's Essays.* New York: Harper and Row Publishers, 1926.

Durgananda, Swami. *The Heart of Meditation.* New York: SYDA Foundation, 2002.

Fillmore, Charles. *Atom Smashing Power of Mind.* Missouri: Unity Books, 1949.

Grimes, John. *A Concise Dictionary of Indian Philosophy.* New York: State of New York University Press, 1989.

Harvey, Andrew. *Teachings of Rumi.* Boston: Shambhala Publications, Inc., 1991.

Hatengdi, M.U. *Nitya Sutras.* Massachusetts: Rudra Press, 1985.

Hawkins, David R. *Power vs. Force.* Carlsbad, California: Hay House, 1995.

Holmes, Ernest. *This Thing Called You.* New York: Penguin Group, 1948.

Isherwood, Christopher. *How to Know God.* Hollywood, California: Vedanta Society of Southern California, 1953.

Khan, Hazrat Inayat. *The Music of Life.* New Lebanon, New York: Omega Publications, 1983.

Khan, Pir Vilayat Inayat. *The Call of the Dervish.* New Mexico: Sufi Order Publications, 1981.

Hafiz and Daniel Ladinsky, translator. *The Gift: Poems by Hafiz.* New York: Penguin Books, 1999: 30, 269.

Lawrence, Brother. *The Practice of the Presence of God.* Fleming H. Revell Co. New Jersey: 1958.

Muktananda, Swami. *Where Are You Going?* SYDA Foundation, New York: 1981.

Muktananda, Swami. *To Know The Knower.* Bombay, SYDA Foundation, South Fallsburg, New York: 1979.

Muktananda, Swami. *Secret of the Siddhas.* South Fallsburg, New York: SYDA Foundation, 1994: 29, 39.

Nirmal Dass. *Songs of Kabir.* New York: State University of New York Press, l991.

Pagels, Elaine. *Beyond Belief.* New York: Random House Inc., 2005.

Ray, Paul and Sherry Anderson. *The Cultural Creatives: How 50 Million People Are Changing the World.* New York: Three Rivers Press, 2000.

Rinpoche, Sogyal. *The Tibetan Book of Living and Dying.* San Francisco: Harper Collins, l992.

Schochet, Jacob. *Tzava'at Harivash.* New York: Kehot Publication Society, 1998.

Simonton, Carl O. and Stephanie Matthew Simonton. *Getting Well Again.* New York: Bantam Books, l978.

Suzuki, D.T. *Zen Buddhism.* New York: Doubleday Anchor Books, 1956.

Talbot, Michael. *The Holographic Universe.* New York: Harper Collins, 1991.

Venkatesananda, Swami, The Concise Yoga Vasistha, State University of New York Press, Albany, 1984.

Yogananda, Paramahansa. *Autobiography of a Yogi.* Los Angeles, California: Self-Realization Fellowship, 1946.

Yukteswar, Sri Swami. *The Holy Science.* Los Angeles: Self-Realization Fellowship, l984.

Acknowledgments

How grateful I am to have had so many loving teachers, beginning in this lifetime with my mother, Geraldine, who ignited my longing for the truth when I was just three. She continued to inspire me throughout her life and beyond.

Thank you to my precious childhood friends who lovingly allowed me to be the "quirky" one among us. Of them I'd especially like to acknowledge Franni Kaupp for her splendid story, Toni Tami for helping with the first draft, and Janine Canan for her invaluable counsel.

Thank you to my two wonderful daughters, Joie and Mia, who trusted me to be their mother, and to my beloved husband, Bruce, who is my best friend and has spiritually supported me for the past forty years.

Thank you to my wisdom teachers, Reverend Darlene Sykes and Reverend Jay Scott Neale who contributed so much to my understanding of scriptural teachings. I treasure the immeasurable gifts of my three Siddha Gurus: Bhagawan Nityananda, Swami Muktananda, and Swami Chidvilasananda, who have given me everything for all lifetimes.

I especially want to thank my computer consultant, Sid Kaplan, for patiently easing me into the computer age, and my editor, Terese Driscoll, who has lovingly guided me with her insights and expertise every step of the way.

Taking the Next Step

For Information go to:

www.beginningsaint.com

Beginning Saint Audio Book
Beginning Saint Curriculum
Calendar of Events
Schedule Speaker
Beginning Saint Bridge Workshops
Individual Beginning Saint Bridge Sessions